THE

100
DAILY HABITS
FOR MORE
SUCCESS,
WEALTH AND
HAPPINESS!

1%

SOLUTION

HOW SMALL DAILY IMPROVEMENTS PRODUCE MASSIVE LONG-TERM RESULTS

EAMONN PERCY

THE 1% SOLUTION

Published and distributed by:
The Ain Group Holdings Ltd.
#196 – 5525 West Boulevard,
Vancouver, BC, Canada
V6M 3W6
Phone: 604-261-6216
percygroup.ca

Contact us at epercy@percygroup.ca for information on author interviews and speaking engagements.

Although the author has made every effort to ensure that the information in this book was correct at press time, the author does not assume, and hereby disclaims, any liability to any party for any loss, damage, or disruption caused by errors or omissions, whether such errors or omissions result from negligence, accident, or any other cause. Some identifying details have been changed to protect the privacy of individuals and organizations. Any slights to individuals or organizations are unintentional. The views and opinions in this book are those of the author. Readers should use their own judgment and consult a qualified professional for advice relating to their specific financial, medical and personal circumstances.

Cover and Interior Design: Yvonne Parks | pearcreative.ca

ISBN 978-0-9950795-0-2

DEDICATION

To my wife Myra and our three wonderful children Loreena,
Katharine and Aidan. Thank you for your love and support.

&

To my brother David, who was the original inspiration for this book
and who encouraged me to share my experiences in order to help
more people achieve their dreams.

TABLE OF CONTENTS

INTRODUCTION

"Human happiness comes not from infrequent pieces of good fortune, but from small improvements to daily life." | Benjamin Franklin

Have you ever noticed how some people seem to consistently make success look easy, while others always seem to struggle? Or how some people have a knack for bouncing back from problems, while others get stuck? Have you seen how, over time, some people you never thought would make it, do, while others who looked promising fell by the wayside?

Over a long enough period of time, life has a way of self-correcting, of balancing our books, of giving us what we truly deserve—though not necessarily what we asked for! The people who make success look easy seem to accomplish more with consistency and poise, while the rest of us seem to struggle.

We want to know their secret: the simple solution that will make problems disappear and dreams come true. The secret to success and the way forward. We believe this secret must exist since we see so many other people making success look easy. We believe there must be something they know that we don't.

We also falsely believe this elusive secret will transform our lives overnight, as if we have arrived at the proverbial end of the rainbow!

1

Whether it's love, money, education, health, career or happiness, we think if we only had the one missing ingredient, then success would be assured. The secret to success seems tantalizingly close, somehow known to everyone but us.

In reality, there is no simple solution. Success comes from the continuous and daily improvement of habits, which compounds to create significant long-term results.

If you study the biographies of successful people, you will find a long history of struggle before significant triumph was ultimately achieved. This explains why the majority of people do not achieve major accomplishments until they are well into adulthood, and often not until the age of 50 or 60, or even beyond.

It takes time, effort and perseverance to develop good disciplines, and then even more time to see the cumulative effect of those disciplines turn into results. While there are methods to accelerate the process, results are achieved by the simple compounding effect of effort and good character, anchored by hard work.

Like water eroding a granite mountainside, or a great cathedral built one brick at a time, the significant accomplishments in life result from doing many small things a little better each day over a long period of time.

The compounding effect of good habits is similar to the compounding effect of money. Imagine the difference if each day you earned $100 and then spent $99, versus earning $100 and spending $101. The first approach, over time, will eventually make you rich. The second approach, over time, will eventually cause you to go broke. The bigger the difference each day, the faster you become rich or the faster you go broke. It's inevitable. It's just math.

Daily improvement has the same long-term, incremental compounding effect. Like money, as the base gets larger and more solid, compounding returns become more substantial. The earlier we start the compounding process, the faster we gain the benefits and the larger the results, until the effect becomes unstoppable.

While there are factors that will have a disproportionate impact on achieving success—such as natural talents, choice of marriage partner, character development, education, career choice, environment and our network—ultimately, good habits rule.

Each day, we need to do many small things well in order to gain the cumulative benefit of efforts.

Ultimately, results are achieved not by doing one thing 100% better each day, but by doing 100 things 1% better each day.

This is The 1% Solution.

This book is about my own journey of continuous improvement. The successes I have enjoyed and the failures that cause me to cringe. It is about the 100 daily habits that have worked for me over the course of this journey, and that I believe will work for you. This book is about giving yourself the opportunity to succeed by focusing on what you can do better, so you can quickly move beyond setbacks, get back on track fast and be better the next day.

I have thoroughly enjoyed writing this book. I hope that, by reading it, you will get the same satisfaction and contentment that I experienced in writing it. This book will give you hope, so that with enough time, you will endure, overcome obstacles, achieve your goals and become the best you can be.

Eamonn Percy

HOW THIS BOOK
WILL HELP YOU

"Live as if you were to die tomorrow. Learn as if you were to live forever." | Mahatma Gandhi

THE PROBLEM THIS BOOK SOLVES

This book solves one of life's biggest problems—*how to overcome a lifetime of obstacles fast enough in order to make a significant impact in the limited time we have or, more precisely, how to become a 20-year overnight success!*

Inside each one of us are big goals and lofty dreams. We aspire to be better people so we can live a fulfilling life, help those we care for, make our mark in this world and leave it a little better than we found it. As humans, we strive for more than just living; we strive to make a difference, to inspire others and to be heroes to our friends and family.

Sometimes we suppress these big aspirations out of fear, since the gap between where we are today and where we hope to be tomorrow looks enormous. Fear can appear to widen this gap, causing us to give up before we even start, or we become discouraged in the process.

5

Discouragement can be compounded by the apparent success of others who, with seemingly less skill and expertise, achieve more.

This book will give you hope. Hope that big dreams can be achieved, hope that a fulfilled life can be lived, hope that your human potential can be realized, hope that the obstacles of today will pale in comparison to the rewards of tomorrow and, finally, hope that you will ultimately be the architect of your future.

How *THE 1% SOLUTION* BENEFITS YOU

The 1% Solution is a simple and easy-to-follow system that will not let you down. It takes a lifetime of daunting effort and breaks it down into bite-sized, daily pieces. It focuses on the certain today, not the uncertain tomorrow. It only requires that you do your best in one 24-hour period, and then let the results of this best daily effort compound to produce a lifetime of progress.

This system is effective since it is based on the principle that makes all great systems work: **simplicity**. Simple, because it only requires *you* to make it successful, it focuses on a *single* day at a time and it helps *prevent* fatal mistakes through daily course correction.

By faithfully following the principles of this book, you will have an effective system that will not let you down and ensures you achieve what is most important. It allows you to put setbacks in perspective and achieve more, without feeling pressured or overwhelmed.

How This Book is Structured

This book has 13 chapters, each representing a theme. I start the beginning of each chapter with a personal anecdote called **My Story**, which illustrates the core concepts of the theme of that chapter. I then follow the anecdote with a number of specific habits, each including a short description and specific actions for implementation.

Each chapter ends with a section called **Actions for Traction**, which summarizes the key points of the chapter, reinforces the concepts with specific recommended actions, and provides space for your thoughts and notes.

There are 100 daily habits in the book, each representing an area of personal improvement. To maximize the value of this book, you should try to practice as many of the 100 habits on as many days as possible.

I end the book with a brief description of a recommended method for improving habits, and provide additional recommended references for your information and additional study.

How to Use This Book

The book can either be read from beginning to end, or used as a reference book by selecting one or two areas for study. However, it is meant to be a companion guide, not a novel, to help you along your way over the rest of your life.

Since we all have unique problems, I designed this book so it can be customized to your specific needs.

Here are three unique ways you can use this book.

First, if you want to improve your overall discipline and habits:

If your long-term goal is personal development, then read the entire book from cover to cover. Concentrate on understanding and implementing *The 1% Solution* as a system, and focus on building the infrastructure and accountability systems necessary to sustain it.

To make the system stick, read one chapter a week. Then focus on implementing the habits in that chapter thoroughly and concentrate on putting them into action. If you read one chapter per week, in 13 weeks you will have read the entire book. Do this three more times and you will have read the entire book four times in one year. This will help improve your discipline tremendously.

Habits can take a long time to change, and require you to consistently focus on enhancing your personal improvement system. If you reinforce good habits by concentrating on a few skills per week, you will significantly increase your probability of success.

SECOND, IF YOU NEED TEMPORARY MOTIVATION:

If you are in a slump and need some encouragement, use *The 1% Solution* as a companion to get through this tough time. Read the introduction and remind yourself that the situation is temporary and it will pass. Focus on action and your best daily effort. Keep this book nearby: in your bag, backpack, office, home or bedside table, and return to it throughout the week. Read through the various sections and focus on the habits that resonate with you the most. Then work on improving those habits the next day. *Reread Chapter 1: A Strong Foundation.*

THIRD, IF YOU WANT TO BUILD A NEW SKILL:

If you find yourself stuck on a specific problem and want to build a new skill to overcome that problem, then focus on improving the one habit that will help you the most. Find the habit that most closely addresses your problem by using the table of contents. Read and study that habit daily for one week.

Discuss the habit with people you know and trust, making notes on how you can implement it well in your own life. Take the actions necessary to make it part of your daily routine. Don't get distracted; stay focused on that habit for at least one full week. If, at the end of one week, you need further reinforcement, then concentrate on the habit again for the second week.

This intensive focus on one habit will help improve your mental state, which will reinforce this habit further while improving your overall discipline and success system. Good habits are like any routine: they cannot exist in isolation. Good habits are supported by good people, good environments and effective systems, which all work together in harmony to produce great results.

WHO AM I TO WRITE ABOUT HABITS?

"Sometimes when you innovate, you make mistakes. It is best to admit them quickly, and get on with improving your other innovations." | Steve Jobs

Like many immigrants seeking a better life, my parents left Europe in the 1950s and came to Canada, where they worked hard to establish a family after giving up everything they had in Ireland. My dad was a hardworking millwright, and my mother lovingly attended to the family of five children while minding the home and working part-time. Both came from a long line of hardworking families in Europe, and now they worked diligently to give their family all the love and advantage they knew we would need to succeed in Canada.

I had a great childhood growing up in Calgary, Alberta, in the 1960s. Later, my parents decided to move to Vancouver, which is where I spent my teenage and early adult years. When we first arrived, we lived in a motel on the strip (Kingsway) in East Vancouver for six months while my parents looked for a home in a good neighborhood. Their hope was to give their children a better life than what they had seen growing up in Ireland during the depression of the 1930s.

We were quickly established in Vancouver, and my parents both worked hard to send me to a very good private boys' school in Grade 7. However, due to my immaturity, I insisted on being moved out of the private school and into the public school system in Grade 10. While I was never strong academically, in the new high school things quickly went from bad to worse. I graduated as a C student with little employment skills and a low probability of advancing my formal education. Before I knew it, I was 19 years old, without prospects, a formal education, career skills or resources, working full-time as a stock boy at a local drugstore.

For several years, I slowly descended into a pattern of undisciplined and unproductive behavior, until one night I literally had an epiphany. *It was a deep and profound experience that made me realize there was no hiding the fact that I was on the wrong track and needed to change my life fast!* The feeling was so intense that I immediately decided to change everything. I let go of all my friends who were a bad influence and set myself five big goals to achieve by the age of 40 (more on that later in the book).

I don't know how, but these goals automatically focused my attention like a laser beam. I immediately embarked on my journey, changed my environment and moved back in with my family (who by this time had moved to Dublin, Ireland) so I could have much-needed structure, discipline and resources.

I then completed a one-year course in electrical and electronics drafting at the Kevin Street College of Technology in Dublin (now part of the Dublin Institute of Technology). After graduation, I returned to Vancouver and started working at a local engineering firm as a draftsman. I was accepted into a two-year electrical and electronics technology program at the British Columbia Institute of Technology (BCIT), and ultimately was accepted into the electrical engineering degree program at Lakehead University, in Thunder Bay, Ontario.

I drove the 1,900 miles from Vancouver to Thunder Bay, sleeping in a car I bought for $55 and put myself through the program, graduating with a B average. It was while I was at Lakehead University that I was fortunate enough to meet my lovely future wife, Myra. I graduated with $30,000 in debt (1986 dollars) and drove home to Vancouver.

In Vancouver, I recalled my earlier high school experience of leaving a promising environment for a poor one and decided to reverse the process by leaving a poor environment for a promising one. I bought a one-way ticket to job-rich Toronto to start my career and landed a job with the Ford Motor Company (Electronics Division) as a Night Shift Production Supervisor at the 1,400-person high-volume advanced automotive electronics manufacturing facility in Markham, Ontario.

At this time, Ford was under considerable competitive pressure, so business innovation and new ideas were highly encouraged and quickly implemented. This environment provided me with the critical foundation necessary for my future business thinking. At night, I completed an MBA at the University of Toronto, Faculty of Management (now the Rotman School of Management).

While at Ford I was recruited to run a Canadian fiber optics plant (which was struggling financially and operationally) that was part of the global company Pirelli. I accepted the role, and led a great management team in the turnaround of the company, going from a significant annual loss to a significant profit, and making the plant one of the best performers for Pirelli worldwide. The basis of the turnaround was what I had learned at Ford: namely, building a culture of merit and performance based upon massive continuous improvements across all aspects of the business.

After Pirelli, I joined Ballard Power Systems, a fast-growing technology company in Vancouver that was in transition from research and development to product development. There, I became Vice President of Operations and helped the company secure new partnerships, technology and resources. During this time, I had the good fortune of working with world-class people and learned a tremendous amount about business and leadership.

After five years at Ballard, I left and started my own business consulting company and grew it for six years before being recruited to run the global utility engineering company Powertech Labs (the for-profit subsidiary of BC Hydro). Working in close cooperation with the Executive Chair, we led the company through a strategic transition, increasing sales and cash dramatically while positioning it for substantial future growth in the fast-growing clean energy/utility engineering market. After 24 years, that would be my last corporate role.

Along the way I had many successes and made a lot of mistakes. However, I never quit moving forward. Meanwhile, my wife and I (to the lesser extent) raised three wonderful children, and we purchased a historic ranch in the beautiful Nicola Valley of British Columbia, Canada, near the world-famous Douglas Lake Ranch.

I decided the second half of my career would be focused on helping other businesspeople by giving back what I had learned during my own executive career about transforming and growing companies. I started by launching a capital and business advisory firm, as well as writing and speaking on the topics of business growth and leadership.

While there were many lessons I have learned so far, there is a single overarching concept that drove all my thinking throughout my professional and personal life, and that continues to do so today. *Continuous improvement and lifelong learning have enabled me to adapt as circumstances changed, so I could overcome difficulties and then progress.*

This growth mindset of lifelong learning was based on the simple premise that we can never go backward; we only thrive by moving forward, however slowly, but always forward and always getting better.

The philosophy of lifelong learning and continuous improvement through the development of good habits, has served me well, and it will serve you well too. If you decide to adopt a mindset of progressing by continuously striving toward a worthy goal, then you will be choosing success on your terms, hope will be at your side and victory will be within your reach.

CHAPTER 1
A STRONG FOUNDATION

"People do not seem to realize that their opinion of the world is also a confession of character." | Ralph Waldo Emerson

MY STORY: AN IMMIGRANT BOY

Each and every one of us has an origin that forms our foundation or roots. Often, it is something experienced when we were young that had a profound and lasting impact. It may have been the influence of our family, parents, culture, environment, religion or friends. In some cases, it was a single experience or significant emotional event that made a fundamental and lasting impression, and other times it was a series of events that left a significant impression.

I was exceedingly fortunate because, while my family was from Ireland, they ultimately made Canada home. We were not wealthy; however, my parents gave us the best that they could afford. More importantly, they also made sure that we had great experiences that shaped our character and thinking.

I truly did everything I could possibly imagine as a young person in order to live those great experiences: sailing, traveling, hiking, summer camps, the proverbial paper route, Air Cadets, Junior Forest Wardens, and many different sports teams. All of these experiences combined together helped me understand myself more fully and appreciate the limitless possibilities in front of me.

In my case, it was not one single event but the combined impact that created a strong foundation. For instance, while being in the Air Cadets taught me discipline, the Junior Forest Wardens taught me about leadership, and team sports taught me cooperation. For several years, I attended Vancouver College (a boys' school in Vancouver, BC, Canada) where the priorities seemed to be sports, religion and academics—in that order! However, with the fullness of time, I saw how well all three disciplines were integrated to support one another, and how all three were critical to the character development of young people at an important age.

One of my most interesting and enjoyable experiences, and my first real taste of making money, was becoming a newspaper delivery boy at the tender age of 12. Every day at 3 pm, right after school finished, I rode my bike to 'The Shack' to pick up my allocation of newspapers to be delivered that day. Rain or shine, people expected their newspapers to be delivered to their doorstep, in good condition and by 5 pm. My job was to deliver, to do it well and to get myself home by 6 pm for dinner. I basically became an independent businessperson, since the business model of the newspaper company for whom I was delivering the papers was effectively to sell the paper to the delivery boys (and a few girls) for distribution, and then make them responsible for collecting money from the customers. At the end of every month, I would start collecting from my customers. I can tell you that, while the amount of money was small, even at that age I quickly learned about human nature, particularly when it came to collecting money! Let me just say that the customers' standards on others for service delivery throughout the month were much higher than the standards they placed on themselves to actually pay for that delivery at the end of the month.

Throughout all of my experiences, both of my parents gave me the love and support that I needed. Even though I drifted in my teenage years, lost my focus and ultimately lost discipline, in retrospect I now realize that those early years gave me a great foundation. The foundation to: live my life with drive, make character a strong priority, understand that it was my life and that I would define success on my own terms and, ultimately, that it was my own responsibility to make something of myself. Nobody was going to do it for me.

So, whatever your own foundational experiences, no matter how diverse, how difficult or strenuous the circumstances, embrace them. Embrace the challenge, embrace your origin, embrace the heartache that made you strong and the dreams that gave you hope. Embrace what made you the unique person you are today. Try to ignore the negative aspects of your early life—put them behind you. If you forget the negatives and build on the positives, you will realize that you already have the foundation necessary to live a positive, important and great life.

HABIT 1

LIVE YOUR LIFE WITH A PURPOSE AND PASSION

"The true soldier fights not because he hates what is in front of him, but because he loves what is behind him." | G.K. Chesterton

In Viktor Frankl's book *Man's Search for Meaning* (Beacon Press, 1959), he describes from his personal experience how some people can endure almost any hardship if their will to live is great enough. While life can be difficult, Viktor Frankl's solution was to find something to live for: *a reason why.* This purpose or reason why needs to be so compelling that it fills us with great passion, so we can drive forward over any and all obstacles, and sustain the will to persevere even through the greatest difficulties.

This purpose fills the void and gives us hope to see a better day, faith that it will arrive, and the courage necessary to make it happen. Our purpose helps us see beyond the daily trials, and reminds us that the sacrifices we make are a small price to pay for achieving something bigger and more important than ourselves. It gives us hope when it is in short supply, and faith when we need it the most.

Take the time to determine what makes you passionate. It may be to provide a better life for your family, give your children more opportunity, make a significant contribution to your community, or achieve a great advancement in business, science, literature or the arts. It can be as grand as leaving a significant financial legacy, or as profound as raising a good family. Passion is personal but makes you powerful. It is meant for you and you alone.

Whatever makes you passionate, let it resonate with every fiber of your being, from your mind to the depths of your soul. Consider it the driver that will propel you forward to achieve your life's work. It is the reason why you do what you do. It gets you up in the morning and keeps you going all day long. Passion will fill you with a sense of accomplishment and pride, knowing that you are becoming a better person and are making a positive impact on others as you strive toward its fulfillment.

While your goals will likely evolve over the course of your life, like seasons in a year, your *reason why* is long-term and visionary. It often strengthens as we mature, becoming stronger as we find our place in the world. As we approach middle age, it often turns to the next generation. And, as we approach the end of our lives, it will focus on our legacy: our desire to leave our mark on the world.

Do not be concerned if you have not yet found that burning desire or purpose. Take the time necessary to determine it; start by writing down what you believe it is. The process of writing always clarifies thinking and becomes a record that can bring focus over time. Don't overanalyze. Instead, listen to the quiet voice inside of you speaking of what is important. This is your calling in life.

Passion should move your thinking to a higher level of consciousness so your mind becomes open to the possibilities. For instance, the accumulation of additional wealth is not that inspirational in itself. However, if you are passionate about earning more to enable your children to get a better education or access to special medical help, your consciousness would determine new ways to make money that you may not normally have considered.

Passion will push you well beyond your comfort zone and will bring forth your gifts in a powerful and meaningful way, making the mark of your time on earth both meaningful and lasting.

HABIT 2

KNOW GOOD CHARACTER AND MAKE IT A PRIORITY

"It is a grand mistake to think about being
great without goodness." | Benjamin Franklin

While purpose defines *why* you live your life, character defines *how* you live it. Good character is a moral compass; so we can do good while achieving more.

When I was building my executive career and had recently become a Vice-President, my boss at the time gave me some great leadership advice. He told me that I would be remembered by the way people felt when I entered the room. I thought this quite curious at the time since I had only been promoted to what I was hoping to be a long and successful executive career, and here he was already talking about me in the past tense! What I did not understand then, and only came to appreciate in the fullness of time, was that he was referring to character building as part of leadership development, not managerial development. I took his advice and try to live it to this day.

We all make poor judgments from time to time, and occasionally do or say the wrong thing. We sometimes think that an apology can cure every unkind word, or that no one will notice our poor behavior.

However, all of these outward expressions are a manifestation of our inner character. Even the smallest lapse, either by commission or omission, is a reflection of our character at that moment. The office supplies taken from work, the undeclared excess change received from a cashier, and the capitulation of a principled stand are not minor lapses in judgment or the result of the vicissitudes of life, but a reflection of our character.

Many of us hold positions of authority. Our work can have a direct impact on the lives of young people who are forming their own character. As adults, we have a significant responsibility to do the right thing all the time, both personally and professionally, to help create more responsible young people and a better society.

While building character is a lifelong endeavor, there are specific actions you can take to be more effective.

Start with Self-Awareness. Self-awareness is critical if you are in a position of authority or leadership. Spend the time necessary to understand your own character traits and flaws, and become in tune with them. Watch your actions and how you rationalize them, being mindful of how you treat others.

Make Character Development a Priority. We review our financial statements regularly, so why not our character statements? By making character development a priority, you not only remind yourself to lead by example, but also to take the actions necessary to have a profound and lasting impact on other people.

Try to Do the Right Thing All the Time. Like most of the great truths of life, this is very easy to say and very hard to do. Reinforce your behavior through constant, spaced and repetitive positive actions.

Over time, good character will become a habit that requires little thought and helps you become a better person. This will ensure that people remember you as a person of integrity who has made a lasting positive impression upon them, helped ease their own burdens, and provided both hope and inspiration when they were most needed.

HABIT 3

DEFINE SUCCESS ON YOUR OWN TERMS

*"The question isn't who is going to let me;
it's who is going to stop me."* | Ayn Rand

We sometimes become confused about whose life we are living. Our own? Our parents? Our friends? Sometimes it seems like everyone else's life but our own.

We are significantly influenced by those closest to us, primarily at a young age, but it continues well into adulthood. Additionally, since we live in a highly interconnected society, media and popular culture can have an unhealthy and major influence on our self-image. Definitions of success can be prescribed through peer pressure, to align behavior more toward peers and less toward the values of the individual.

Hyper-consumption can define success as material possessions, driving us to feel inadequate, or encouraging poor financial habits.

Well-meaning friends and family can have their own definitions of success, and wish to see us fit closer to their perceptions, rather than ours.

Parents and schools often define success in terms that were adequate for their own generation, but completely inadequate for the future generation that today's students will face.

I believe you need to define success on your own terms! Not on the terms of your parents, society, friends, family, or even your spouse, but on the terms that work for you, and you alone. They must be terms that work for your current circumstances and capabilities of today, and your plans for tomorrow.

By defining success on your own terms, you disregard the expectations of others and create milestones upon which you can build the habit of achievement. By defining success on your own terms, you can become your own winner, not someone else's loser. If you fail, you can try again, with more knowledge and experience to aid you. If you succeed, you meet your own expectations, not those of others.

I am not advocating making life too easy or setting the bar too low, but making sure you create the right environment for yourself to become successful so you can build the habits, motivations and rewards necessary to achieve your own goals and become the winner you are meant to be.

To define success on your terms, do the following:

Define What Success Means to You. Be thoughtful when you consider success and put real meaning to it. Think beyond career, material possessions and the external world. Focus inward on self-development and on being the best you can be, so you can magnify your impact and help more.

Determine Why You Want to Achieve It. Ask "Why?" a lot, and try to understand what drives you. Look at your external world for influence, positive and negative, and seek to understand the source of your motivation. Be thoughtful, introspective and deliberate.

Have the Courage to Say It's Important and Stay the Course. Have the courage to stand up to the forces around you and be your own person, a free individual with free will. Build the character muscle necessary to determine what success will mean to you, and then build the perseverance necessary to achieve it.

HABIT 4

FOCUS ON YOUR INTENTION

"Whether you think you can or you think you can't,
you are right." | Henry Ford

Too often, we focus on what we want to avoid, rather than on our intention. This is a natural human behavior, but a very disruptive one, since whatever we focus on materializes. If we focus on negative people and things, then the universe conspires to send us more negative people and things. If we focus on positive people and things, that is what we tend to get.

Have you ever had the experience of driving and notice a distraction or obstacle, and the more you focus on it the more you tend to be drawn to it? If you go to a good driving school, they will always remind you to look where you want to go, and the car will be pulled in the direction of your focus.

Similarly, have you ever been in a group conversation where someone brings up a slightly negative topic, like the poor weather for instance, and within minutes everyone is talking about the negative subject? We get more of whatever we focus on. That's the way our brains are wired.

Get into the habit of focusing on your intention and how to achieve it. Ultimately, this is the best way to stay motivated over a long period of time. Be constantly mindful of what is the most important thing to achieve. By focusing on that intention, you can move significant forces (both internal and external) in your world in order to make it happen.

Here are four practical tips on how to focus on your intention:

Avoid All Negativity at All Times. Don't talk about it, don't think about it, and don't let anyone near you be negative. Treat it like a virus that must be avoided for you to stay alive. Negativity will crowd out your intention.

Write Down Your Goals Daily. This simple act will reinforce your intention in your mind and will help you stay focused on what's important. It takes less than one or two minutes to write down your most important goals.

Eliminate Excessive Media. Seriously consider going on a *media detox* by disconnecting the TV, turning off all devices for the evening and eliminating most media from your life. This will remove the clutter from your thinking and let you focus on what's most important.

Focus on How You Are Going to Achieve Your Intentions. Do this so you are not only focused on what you want to achieve, but also on how you're going to achieve it. Break your intention down into bite-sized pieces, so you can determine what you need to do today, tomorrow and going forward in order to achieve that goal.

ACTIONS FOR TRACTION

What three character traits do you value most?

_____

_____

_____

How can you put these character traits into action this week?

_____

_____

_____

Who will help you improve your habits and why?

_____

_____

_____

Describe your foundational habits. Why are they important?

_____

_____

_____

CHAPTER 2
BEING GOOD

"Character cannot be developed in ease and quiet. Only through experience of trial and suffering can the soul be strengthened, ambition inspired, and success achieved." | Helen Keller

My Story: The Friday Night Club

When I was in Grade 6, one of my good friends invited me to join a youth group called The Friday Night Club. I always thought it was great marketing, since who in Grade 6 wouldn't love to go to a group called The Friday Night Club? I joined the club and thought it was fantastic! Every Friday night, a group of us would get together at the local school and play all the games that children of that age love (particularly dodgeball). After an evening of playing games, we would sit down and drink hot chocolate while a few of the group leaders would bring out guitars and play some songs. (It was the 1970s, after all!)

The real highlight of The Friday Night Club was the annual Easter trip to a camp on Anvil Island, near Vancouver. It was three days of adventure, with the highlight being a sauna, followed by jumping on a 50-foot slide that went from the top of a rocky bluff into the cold water of the Pacific Ocean. My next favorite activity was playing a game called Moon Ball. The objective was for one team to push this gigantic five-foot-high ball against the opposing team from one end of the field to the other. Absolute mayhem erupted every single time.

As I got older, I continued going to both the camp and the Friday night games. However, with time, both slowly morphed from games to group discussion, and from discussion to thinking. By the time I was in Grade 9, dodgeball time had turned into a study group and I was thinking more about my young life. My parents had always made character development a priority, particularly related to being honest, treating people with respect and telling the truth; however, this study group was different.

I remember the impact I felt by reading and studying *Hinds' Feet on High Places* (Wilder, 2010) by Hannah Hurnard, which is an allegorical story about overcoming fear and the daily struggle to live a good life. What I did not know from the experience at the time, and I can see now in retrospect, was that I was learning about life, and just in time; I was entering the tumultuous teenage years and could see dark clouds on my horizon.

I was learning the importance of being good at a critical age in my life. I was learning to embrace difficulty, I was learning about character, I was learning about respect, integrity and commitment—not only from my family, but more importantly, I was also learning it in an environment with other young people my age.

Like most of the great truths of life, we don't know we are learning the lesson at the moment. It's not until the fullness of time that we appreciate the core value of the lesson. For me, this was only the first step of striving to be good as I matured. However, unbeknownst to me, the seed had been planted at an early age, with the benefits following decades later.

HABIT 5

LEAD BY GOOD CHARACTER EXAMPLE DAILY

"Example is not the main thing in influencing others.
It is the only thing." | Albert Schweitzer

Young children first mimic their parents' behavior in order to please, then to learn, then to practice and then to be. They watch how their parents eat, dress, carry themselves and treat others. This mimicking eventually becomes their own adult habits. *They learn which values their parents hold most important by watching their actions, not by listening to their words.*

In the work environment, the actions of the leader eventually become the culture of the organization. Those actions are largely defined by the leader's character, especially by his or her small, unconscious acts throughout the day. As a leader, even your smallest action is judged by those around you. Over time, actions come to represent the larger picture of your character, which is reflected back to you by the organization.

Developing the habit of *leading by example* is one of the most powerful ways to reinforce your own good habits while helping those around you. You get the benefit of the initial good action, which reinforces your habits, and the additional benefit of the feedback from those you are leading, which guides your continued improvement.

By focusing on your own daily *leadership by example*, you place responsibility for your own character development in one place— your shoulders. You accept responsibility for those you are leading, who may not have achieved the same level of personal development as you have. *Leading by example* requires resolve and steadfast commitment, as you must hold yourself to a very high standard.

Use the following steps to make *leadership by example* a part of your daily routine:

Remind Yourself Who You Are Leading. Whether at home, work, school or in the community, all of us are in some form of leadership role. Each day, ask yourself who is watching you, who are you teaching, why are they important to you and what impact do you want to have on them? This will help your resolve to be better.

Keep Good Character Traits in the Forefront of Your Mind. Focus on interactions with others in areas where you can demonstrate respect, empathy, humility, fortitude and courage.

To aid in your character development, here is a list of the *10 Principles of Good Character*, according to the book *Character Matters* (Touchstone, 2004) by Dr. Thomas Lickona, the Developmental Psychologist and Professor of Education at the State University of New York at Cortland, where he directs the Center for the Fourth and Fifth Rs (Respect and Responsibility).

10 Principles of Good Character

1. Wisdom (Good Judgment)

2. Justice (Golden Rule)

3. Fortitude (Inner Toughness)

4. Self-Control

5. Love (Sacrifice for Others)

6. Positive Attitude

7. Hard Work

8. Integrity (Honesty with Yourself)

9. Gratitude

10. Humility (Desire to Be Better)

Seek Out Opportunities to Exhibit Good Character. Do not shy away from a difficult situation, since that is where we often become our best, particularly if it involves helping others. Be very mindful during critical or emotional episodes, which often call upon us to dig deepest into the character pool, and are exceptional opportunities to build character.

Follow the Example of Great Leaders You Admire. Find ways to emulate their behavior and understand how they made character development a critical aspect of their own lives. Then make it part of your own daily routine.

Build a Culture of Character in Your Home and Workplace. It's your actions that set the tone and culture of an organization, not your words. Encourage truthfulness, honesty and a no-spin environment. Create an environment where it is safer to speak the truth, no matter how unpleasant, than it is to hide behind nuance and deception. Do this by bringing problems to the forefront and by being brave, focusing on what you learn from failing and to trying again with better knowledge.

Leading with good character example each day puts the entire emphasis on yourself for improvement. Be open, honest and humble by admitting your mistakes and by actively seeking out feedback from people who will help you understand your weaknesses and fix them permanently.

HABIT 6

KEEP YOUR ACTIONS ALIGNED WITH YOUR VALUES

"Whoever is careless with the truth in small matters cannot be trusted with important matters." | Albert Einstein

Every day we are faced with countless small decisions. While each one individually is not critical, they do add up over time. However, it is not possible or logical to stop and consider each small decision prior to its execution. Therefore, we must rely on something else to help guide these decisions to ensure they are consistent with our overall mission in life, our character development and our progress toward achieving goals. This 'something else' is our *values*.

Our values are the set of attributes that we think are most important in our lives. They guide all aspects of our life, from major decisions such as a marriage partner or career to minor daily decisions. *Values* are usually developed when we are young, and they frame our world view and drive behavior. Some examples of values are trust, hopefulness, respect, altruism, security and integrity.

By clearly understanding your *values* and how they were formed, you will gain perspective on why you make certain decisions and gravitate toward certain people or circumstances, whether or not they are aligned with your long-term goals.

Understand and clarify your *values* through self-reflection, asking those whom you trust or using more structured analytical methods. There are many excellent tools available for this purpose, such as the Myers-Briggs Type Indicator, Insights Discovery, etc.

Write your *values* down and then ask yourself these questions:

- Are these truly what I value most in my life?
- Is my life's purpose aligned with these *values*?
- Are my actions aligned with these *values*?
- If so, how do I reinforce these actions daily?
- If not, how do I change my actions until they are aligned?

Once this exercise is complete, make a conscious effort each day to eliminate the actions and small behaviors that are inconsistent with your *values*. I have found it much easier to make changes to small daily behaviors than to large lifelong behaviors.

You may find the following examples useful:

- If you value trust and are a business leader, give an employee the benefit of the doubt more frequently, even it means there may be an occasional minor misstep or setback. This will become an opportunity for them to learn.
- If you value productivity, then lead by example rather than by always expecting it from others. Be the first person in the office in the morning and the last to leave at night.

- If you value tolerance or respect, then give someone else the opportunity to state an opinion, particularly if it differs from your own, and let it stand.

These small daily actions and decisions will accumulate over a lifetime, helping you develop a set of values consistent with the achievement of your long-term goals, ultimately making progress enjoyable to pursue and easier to achieve.

HABIT 7

ASSOCIATE WITH PEOPLE YOU ASPIRE TO BE LIKE

"Associate yourself with men of good quality if you esteem your own reputation; for 'tis better to be alone than in bad company." | George Washington

Habits are often difficult to form or difficult to break because they get reinforced daily by our environment, emotion and people around us. Motivational speaker Jim Rohn famously said, "We are the average of the five people we spend most of our time with." If you believe this, as I do, then it vastly simplifies the task of habit development. If you want to be a certain way, simply associate more with people who are that way. Want to be fit? Associate with fit people. Want to be rich? Associate with rich people. Want to be happy? Associate with happy people!

So, if it is so simple, why don't more people actually do it?

There are three reasons. First, many people don't know what they want, so they dabble and drift, ultimately ending up with people who also don't know what they want. Second, fear of change and comfort with the status quo, which keeps us with the current clique we know, can hold us back from meeting new people and forming new relationships. Finally, many people don't know how to make new associations and personal bonds. That's where I can help.

Here is what you do:

Focus on Creating Value First. No one wants to associate with people who consume precious resources: they are numerous and easy to find. We all want to spend time with people who create resources and enrich our lives in meaningful ways. You can create value for others by offering to save them time, make them money, decrease their risk, raise their profile or contribute to a cause important to them. Be creative!

Take Initiative and Make the First Contact. Don't wait for someone to roll out the red carpet; otherwise, you will be waiting a long time. The internet and social media are making it easier than ever to connect with people. Don't forget to pick up the phone and just call, too. Try to find a referral or a point of common interest prior to making contact with a new person, and script the conversation so you have notes to fall back upon if you get flustered.

Be Clear in Your Intention. Know precisely why you want to associate with certain people, what you intend to achieve and what you intend to give in return. For instance, when I finished my corporate career, I realized I needed much more experience in the entrepreneurial and start-up world, so I joined a local technology accelerator as a CEO-in-Residence. I was exposed to hundreds of companies and entrepreneurs over a two-year period and I intensely coached about 30 companies.

Think Globally. It is a big world out there. Find kindred spirits and networks of like-minded people whom you admire. This gives you much greater reach, and the added benefit of cultural, ethnic, geographic and social diversity. In addition, you can very precisely target people who have skill sets and interests that align with your own. Most people will certainly do you the courtesy of listening to your pitch to connect in some way, particularly if they see the value in it.

Don't Quit. Your quest to find like-minded people is a lifelong pursuit. It will require you to let go of some behaviors and people in your life now in order to make room for other behaviors and people in the future. This is a normal part of continuous improvement. By sticking to it and following the suggestions above, you will make a habit out of connecting with people who raise your average performance, moving you from good to great, and your results from middle-class to world-class.

HABIT 8

FOLLOW THE GOLDEN RULE

"If you want to lift yourself up, lift up someone else." | Booker T. Washington

The Golden Rule states that we should do unto others as we would have them do unto us. This is the foundation of many great religions and natural laws.

If you believe that most people are genuinely good, as I do, then this is a great starting point for building a long-term relationship. There are definitely cases where you will be disappointed, for a variety of reasons, but that can be dealt with over time. As a starting point, following the Golden Rule will form the basis of trusted, long-term and important relationships.

Reciprocity is a natural human condition, likely rooted in our early evolutionary history where we depended heavily on other members of our immediate clan for daily survival. There is a tremendous amount of science to show that reciprocity works. Read *Influence: The Psychology of Persuasion* (William Morrow and Company, 1991) by Robert B. Cialdini for more information. In his research on influence, Cialdini found that people are hardwired to return a favor or gift. We literally cannot help ourselves. I think he found the basis for the *Golden Rule*, or even karma.

So, following the Golden Rule is not only the right thing to do, but the science also proves that it works. We get what we give. Give a compliment, get one back. Give a gift, get one back. Give a favor, get one back.

Building the habit of following the Golden Rule requires a daily willingness to be authentic and take risks in a relationship. It means being open to a positive relationship, without being too trusting, since trust requires evidence built over time. The Golden Rule is the starting point of relationships, but not necessarily the ending point. However, more often than not, treating people with kindness, consideration, and care will be reciprocated in equal or greater proportion, helping you build the self-confidence and support needed to achieve big and important goals.

HABIT 9

BUILD MENTAL FORTITUDE

"Fortitude is the marshal of thought, the armor of the will, and the fort of reason." | Francis Bacon

Like any significant project, starting is easy, but the finishing is hard. Pick your favorite project: parenting, health, wealth, education or business, and it's the same model of an eager start, a slow climb and a tremendous push to the finish. In the end, anything worth doing is very, very hard, which is why so many people quit before accomplishing true greatness. They run out of steam and let the obstacles overcome them, rather than overcoming the obstacles.

While there are a number of factors that go into making a person persist until they succeed, I believe the most important factor is a high degree of fortitude or mental toughness. *Fortitude is the ability to generate mental courage or strength in the face of difficulty, danger or extreme adversity.* It's grit, resolve or backbone. It's the willingness to go beyond fear into the unknown, with confidence. It's not about being reckless; rather, it's facing fear with the inner conviction that you will succeed.

To build fortitude in your life, try the following:

Remind Yourself of Your Duty and Purpose. Mine is to fulfill my personal potential in order to create abundance for those I care about most, my family. By reminding myself of why I am pursuing a goal, I create a higher calling, which makes my obstacles seem smaller in comparison. This approach lengthens my time horizon, since my purpose is multigenerational, and reduces the timeline of the obstacle. For instance, if your goal is to stay healthy to be a role model for your family over a generation, it becomes less difficult to work out for only 45 minutes every day. When you encounter adversity, remind yourself of your purpose.

Build Reserves of Fortitude Before You Need Them. Test or challenge yourself regularly, particularly if you start to get too comfortable or backslide. Set your own challenge, great or small, and build your fortitude muscle.

Persist Well Beyond the Rational or Reasonable Level for a Project. I do this because I have learned over my career that truly great businesses and business leaders are rarely reasonable or rational. They can't be, since the business world is unreasonable and the rate of change can be irrational. These great entrepreneurs think in exponential and accelerated terms, and change their world around them, rather than being changed by it. You can do this by adopting big goals, associating with exceptional people, pushing for excellence when it's required, and by trying to find an unconventional way around or through an obstacle. While it does not always succeed, the effort itself build fortitude and resolve.

Don't try to change your world in one day. Rather, focus on building fortitude, or inner toughness, which will serve you during difficult times, and be an inspiration for those you care for.

BUILD AND LIVE YOUR PERSONAL BRAND REPUTATION

"The way to gain a good reputation is to endeavor to be what you desire to appear." | Socrates

How often have we held certain feelings toward someone without really understanding why? Those feelings or perceptions are the brand reputation you associate with that person, and result from all of your interactions with them over time. They can be feelings of love, trust, integrity and hard work, or of deceit, mistrust and pain. Whatever they are, we unconsciously are creating our brand every moment of the day through the little things we think, say and do.

These little daily thoughts, words and actions build our self-image, which ultimately manifests itself as outward actions. Over time, people reflect these actions back upon us, reinforcing our self-image and personal brand. Product brands are skillfully crafted to project a certain image in the marketplace, for the sole purpose of creating enduring value. Keep these same goals in mind when creating your personal brand.

A great personal brand can significantly leverage your efforts and magnify your accomplishments, as people will have a higher level of certainty in you by trusting your brand; therefore, this enables you to accomplish more in less time and with less effort. Your brand will precede you, enabling others to confidently recommend you or your services, knowing that you will not only deliver, but your strong brand will enhance them as well. Finally, a strong personal brand is a great way of reinforcing our own behaviors, as it provides a reference point against which we can benchmark our actions throughout the day.

Here's how to build and maintain a superior personal brand:

Make a Short List of the Character Traits that You Feel Are Most Important in Your Personal Brand. Write them down and read them daily. Remind yourself why they are important and seek to live those traits in all of your interactions.

Seek the Right Environment. Keep the company of people who will reinforce your personal brand and enable you to focus on your strengths, thereby making it easier to live your brand promise.

Invest in Your Personal Brand. Make a commitment to personal development, educational advancement and top-quality infrastructure for the home and office, and then invest strategically in those areas. This will give you a lifetime return on your hard-earned personal brand.

Recall that a Reputation Takes a Lifetime to Build and Only a Moment to Lose. Try to avoid those situations that can destroy your personal brand, particularly in this age of instant and mass communication, social media and digital sharing.

Reputation is truly your own and can be the single biggest factor that contributes to success in health, wealth and family. Why? Because your reputation is what determines how others both perceive you and decide to work with you, before any actual interaction with you. It is the great invisible lever that can leave you on the ground or lift you to great heights.

ACTIONS FOR TRACTION

What is your strongest character trait? How did you develop it?

_____

_____

_____

What is your weakest character trait? How can you improve it?

_____

_____

_____

Who are some leaders you admire and why?

_____

_____

_____

What is the one thing you can do today to make character development a higher priority in your life?

_____

_____

_____

CHAPTER 3

ACHIEVING GOALS

"First, have a definite, clear practical idea; a goal, an objective.
Second, have the necessary means to achieve your ends; wisdom,
money, materials, and methods. Third, adjust all your
means to that ends." | Aristotle

MY STORY: THE EPIPHANY

When I was young, I was never particularly goal-oriented. While I had some rough ideas as to what I wanted to do with my life, anything beyond age 20 was a fog. I was focused on enjoying my youth. It was not until I was beyond the tumultuous years of high school did I start to see the value of setting goals.

My high school years were challenging. They started off well, as my parents had the insight to enroll me in a very good private boys' school in Vancouver. I knew it was a financial stretch for them to make it happen. Being immigrants, they understood the importance of a good education and wanted a better life for my siblings and me. While I started the private school in Grade 7, it was not until Grade 8 that I began to feel I was not strong academically and the school was not a good fit for me. As I progressed into Grade 9, these feelings grew. So, even though my parents had done a lot to get me into a very good school and were making financial sacrifices to keep me there, I told them that I wanted to withdraw and go to the local public school for Grade 10.

They agreed to my request, but after the move, things went downhill fast. The academic expectations in the new school were low, accountability was low, discipline was low and, as a result, my performance was low. Unsurprisingly, I did not thrive. By the time I finished high school, I had a C average, very little prospects, hardly any skills, and few of the disciplines required for future success.

With no prospects, I took a variety of odd jobs and ended up a year later working the midnight shift as a stock boy at the local drugstore in Vancouver. I have very vivid memories of arriving at work at 11 pm each night, where my job was to unload a 40-foot tractor-trailer filled with boxes of tissues, toilet paper, baby food and diapers, and then stock the store shelves with these staples of family life. Every night became the same thing: unload the truck, stock the shelves and clean up the mess before customers arrived in the morning. To top it off, my entire family had moved back to Ireland to start a business, and I was living in a room and board arrangement with a family friend. If you ever want to get motivated to make more money or improve your career, work a midnight shift of any job for a few weeks and your motivation to change will go through the roof! This became my life.

After a year of this, my father visited from Ireland, saw the state that I was in, and took me back with him to help me get on the straight and narrow. When I was there, he highly encouraged me, as any good father would, to enroll in a one-year Electrical Drafting course at the Kevin Street College of Technology, which I took in order to improve my job prospects. At the end of one year, having finished the course,

I decided to go back home to Vancouver to get a job, as Ireland in the early 1980s was an economic basket case. I was able to get a job as an electrical draftsman with a prominent local engineering company and started to earn a reasonable income. However, I still lacked a formal education and the prospects necessary to build the type of life that I wanted—all because I did not have significant goals.

After working as a draftsman for a few months, and now two years since graduating from high school, I attended a party one night with a number of my high school friends. Several of them were rapidly completing engineering degrees from various top universities in Ontario, and they spent the night talking about what they would do with their new degrees. The difference between their bright futures and my sorry state was so stark that I literally had an epiphany (a moment of profound insight). *I was struck by insight in a deep, spiritual and profound way. I realized at that very moment that I was at a fork in the road and that if I didn't do something significant very quickly, I would soon be left behind.*

I immediately left the party and went home. I decided to let go of all the people in my life who were negative, holding me back, and not aligned with a better future. Instead, I vowed to embrace the people who were positive and who could help me move forward. **I set myself five major goals to be achieved by the age of 40.** They were:

1. To get an electrical engineering degree and an MBA
2. To be happily married and have three children
3. To run a company
4. To buy a home in Vancouver
5. To become financially secure

These goals seemed outrageous at the time, given that I was living in one room, with no formal education, no job prospects, no family connections, no resources and no money. But I gave myself these goals because I needed to do something significant, something big and something that could massively change my life.

I immediately embarked upon achieving these goals. The first thing I did was enroll in the local college called British Columbia Institute of Technology (BCIT). I did this because I had heard that there was only one electrical engineering school in Canada (Lakehead University) that allowed 100% of the college credits to be applied against university engineering credits. In essence, I knew I could get the full four-year engineering degree done by taking two years at BCIT and two years at Lakehead. I loved the idea of actually getting into an engineering school by going through the college, doing it quickly and cost-effectively.

I took a remedial math course as a condition of acceptance into BCIT, as I had only Grade 10 math at the time. Once I started, I quickly realized how poor my academic skills actually were. There were a number of occasions where I barely made it through the program and was a few percentage points away from failing completely. In order to apply to Lakehead University, I needed a 75% minimum grade-point average (GPA). This doesn't sound like a high bar, but given my previous academic performance and the difficulty of the program, I found it quite challenging. I decided to focus 100% of my intention on increasing my average, so I took two index cards and wrote the number 76% on each of them. I taped one in front of my desk at home, and one to the middle of my car's steering wheel. Each day I would focus on those numbers, knowing that this was what I needed to achieve. After two hard years at BCIT, I was very pleased to find out that I had achieved 76%, and I had the necessary grades to apply to Lakehead University. I had dropped 33 pounds while at BCIT due to the extreme physical and mental stress of completing the program. However, I had achieved an important step toward my first big goal.

This whole experience had a profound impact on me. For the first time in my adult life, I had seen the effect of focusing on and achieving important goals, and I knew that I could do this for the rest of my life. All of a sudden, big goals did not seem to be so unachievable, and I knew I could do more.

HABIT 11

ALWAYS THINK BIG

"Faith is daring to put your dream to the test. It is better to try to do something and fail than to try to do nothing and succeed." | Robert Schuller

Like most things in our lives, the size of our thinking is simply a habit. Small thinking is destructive, time-consuming and a waste of human potential for three reasons:

1. By thinking small, we are not pushing the boundaries of what may be possible.

2. We infect those around us, often the people we care most about, with little thoughts which may limit others from accomplishing great things.

3. Small thinking robs us of the big obstacles and massive challenges that are a necessary part of personal growth.

I love the concept of thinking big because it is among the few tools we have to change our mental perspectives, which ultimately drives all of our actions. Thinking big opens up new possibilities that may have always been in front of us, but that we could not see. It removes mental blinders and massively broadens our views of the world.

Developing the habit of thinking big requires breaking the habit of thinking average, changing your perspective and replacing it with a new habit. It takes awareness of the problem, a shift in thinking, the development of new habits and the reinforcement of those new habits.

To think big, do the following:

Be Aware of Your Thinking. Watch yourself throughout the day. Become a third party to your own actions and look for those triggers that may cause you to think small. For instance, you may be engaged in small thinking related to money habits, or under the influence of certain friends or family members, or when doing something for yourself or your career. The key is to be self-aware of what is driving the small thinking.

Change Your Perspective. Look for ways to massively change your perspective and then act. Go somewhere new or different, dine at new and better restaurants, travel more, take different routes on your commute, find new social circles or join a new club. Actively seeking new perspectives will break the patterns of the past while making new connections for future thinking.

Ask "What If?" and "Why Not?" Drop cynicism and the "It won't work…" or "I've tried that…" mentality. Instead, ask "What if…?" and "Why not…?" more often. These new questions will open your mind to the possibilities. It may start modestly, but you will quickly find that thinking big becomes a habit. Think growth. Think abundance. Double your sales goals, train for a marathon, start writing a book—anything at all that changes your thinking or perspective. Ask yourself "Why not me and why not now?"

Reinforce the Thinking Big Habit. It is critical to surround yourself with people who will lift your thinking to a higher level. This will reinforce your new behavior and prevent backsliding.

Don't wait for an opportunity to think big to come along. Try to do something big each and every day, and you will earn the pride that comes from achieving big goals and doing something worthwhile for those you love.

HABIT 12

DETERMINE YOUR DEFINITE PURPOSE

*"Definiteness of purpose is the starting point
of all achievement."* | W. Clement Stone

Napoleon Hill's classic book, *Think and Grow Rich* (The Ralston Society, 1937) is one of my favorite books of all time. His work is based on a 25-year study of 250 of the most successful businesspeople of his generation. He has truly collected, analyzed and synthesized the success strategies of some of the most amazing people in modern history and summarized it for us in simple book form. He outlines the proven, clear and methodical steps necessary to achieve success. I highly recommend it.

The first principle of success he mentions is to create a *definite purpose*. In other words, before you get started on your own journey, determine exactly where you are going, what you want to achieve and why you want to achieve it. He didn't name it a fuzzy vision or a consideration; he calls it a *definite purpose*! A precise and clear definition of what you want to achieve.

This idea has always appealed to me, since we all need a reason to live and something that gets us fired up each day. Otherwise, we are drifting, at best going nowhere, often regressing. I would much rather be moving toward something better, clear and concrete every day, than drifting and looking back.

WHAT IS YOUR DEFINITE PURPOSE?

If you don't have one, take the time to write one down now. I am not talking about goals, but the overall intention that drives you forward every day, fills you with pride, and causes you to dig deep during the times of trouble and sacrifice. The definite purpose is the beacon you see off in the distance every day that you move toward, rarely in a straight line, but it guides your overall direction of all your resources, effort and time.

Examples of a definite purpose include: raising children of character who become contributing members of society, building a business to a value of $100 million so that half of that can be given away to important causes later in life, building an academic career that significantly advances the boundary of existing knowledge, being awarded a Nobel Prize or becoming the best parent you can possibly be.

Keep your definite purpose short, but exciting. Write it down where it can be seen or read daily, and make it part of your ritual. Make it real and keep it at the front of your mind each day until its visualization and achievement become a reality.

HABIT 13

SET MASSIVE ANNUAL GOALS THAT INSPIRE ACTION

"If you don't know where you are going, any road will get you there." | Anonymous

In order to succeed and to move to a higher level, we must focus on great achievement that constantly pushes us forward. This focus comes from one source: *persistent effort toward the achievement of worthy goals.* As goal-seeking beings, this resonates with a deep inner and evolutionary desire. Humans are hardwired to progress.

Setting annual goals is a great way to make this happen. The cycle of one year is a good milestone to measure progress, and the beginning of the year is a time of renewal—out with the old and in with the new. Twelve months is also about the right length of time to accomplish something significant, enabling us to move the needle quickly with sustained effort.

I personally have been setting annual goals every year for more than 25 years and have found it to be critical to helping me build family, career, wealth, happiness and other accomplishments. I owe much to this one simple habit.

I have learned that it takes five key things to make annual goal-setting both productive and successful. They are:

1. **Set Goals that Are in Complete Alignment with Your Lifetime Definite Purpose.** Your annual goals should be the critical short-term steps that must be accomplished in order to achieve your bigger lifetime purpose. It's easier to achieve your definite purpose when you break it down into concrete, attainable annual steps.

2. **Establish Goals that Are Both Important and Exciting.** While many important tasks are tough and boring, they are critical to your long-term success and need to be included in your goals. However, ensure you also have the goals that excite you and get your adrenaline pumping. This will keep you inspired to take action and move toward bigger accomplishments and a better life.

3. **Don't Spend a Lot of Time Creating Your Goals.** I only commit an hour or two to setting my annual goals since I don't want to overthink them. I usually have a very good idea of what I need to do anyway, as I have been thinking about them through the year.

4. **Make Goals that Seem Unattainable at the Time.** Don't worry initially about how you are going to achieve your goals; that will come. Focus only on outcomes that will make your life massively better. This will move your thinking to a higher level and help you access capabilities and resources that you didn't know you had. If you knew it was easy and how to accomplish it, you likely would have done it by now.

5. **Write Your Goals Down.** Talk is cheap. Most serious commitment happens in writing (pledges, contracts, etc.). Write your goals down, along with target dates for their accomplishment. Sign the document and post it somewhere you can read it several times a day. This will remind you of its importance and help you stay on track. Even better, write out your goals every morning. This will reinforce them in your mind and make their accomplishment more likely.

HABIT 14

ONLY DISCUSS YOUR GOALS WITH COLLABORATORS

"There is only one way to avoid criticism:
do nothing, say nothing, and be nothing." | Aristotle

It's natural and healthy to feel enthusiastic about setting goals and deciding to make a meaningful and important change in our lives. Usually, our first instinct is to tell someone since we hope that they will feel as good about the goals as we do. Often, we start telling the people we are closest to, either friends, family or workmates, with little or no consideration given to how enthusiastic they are about **us achieving our goals**.

After sharing our goals, we often get a positive response, or at least a neutral one, which encourages us so we continue the practice. A few people will be extremely negative or try to discourage us. However, many will offer a few words of encouragement but inwardly may hold other feelings. Their actions are different from their words; since they will inwardly see no upside for themselves, they are unlikely to help you.

Think about it. If there is nothing in it for them, why would they want you to achieve your goals? In many cases, your achievement of these goals puts these people in a worse situation. Will your work colleagues want to see you get promoted? Do your friends want to see you with a bigger house or traveling to exotic places more often without them? Does your extended family want to see you become very wealthy while they don't?

Achieving massive goals and making progress results in one thing— change! Change can be good or bad depending on your point of reference. If you are improving, your point of reference shows progress. If someone else is improving and you are not, or you are not progressing as quickly, your point of reference shows regression. For instance, picture an expensive convertible speeding down the street. The driver feels exhilaration, excitement, the wind in her hair and forward momentum. Meanwhile, someone in a slower car sees the convertible passing, its back end disappearing into the distance. One speeding car, two different points of reference.

Be extraordinarily careful with whom you share your goals, dreams and aspirations. Only share them with people in complete alignment with their achievement: usually a spouse, business partner, employee, trusted friend or close family member.

There is no value in telling those close to you when they are not supportive; it can even be detrimental to your own progress. Come from a place of love and say nothing while keeping a warm relationship with those you love. They generally mean no harm; they just want to see you in a way that suits them, not you. The resulting harmony and positive energy will be good for your own life and helpful in keeping good, long-term, warm relationships, while you seek and find those who are in true alignment with the accomplishment of your goals.

HABIT 15

USE ACCELERATORS TO GET THERE MORE QUICKLY

"When everything seems to be going against you, remember that the airplane takes off against the wind, not with it." | Henry Ford

George Bernard Shaw once said, "Youth is wasted on the young!" It's true, not because young people don't necessarily appreciate the abundance they have, but because they don't appreciate the time they have remaining to grow it.

We all like to think that we have an ample amount of time to accomplish everything we wish in our lives. The reality is quite different. We often underestimate the amount of time, and effort, involved in truly accomplishing great goals since we likely haven't done it before. Many of us waste what little time we do have in the pursuit of meaningless pastimes, trivia, time-wasters and low-value activities.

Later in life, our responsibilities seem to increase in direct proportion to the decrease in time available. Renowned Canadian entrepreneur and philanthropist Joe Segal refers to this declining balance as "the runway of life." Our lifespan is finite and, just like a runway, it will come to an end. There is no extension, or extra time, or second life to live. *This is truly it!*

Consequently, it's important to be wise with the limited time you have and avoid time-consuming people and activities. This will make an enormous difference in your life and immediately free you up to achieve greater productivity and focus throughout your day. While this alone won't give you sufficient time to accomplish your most important goals, time-wasters should be thoroughly eliminated from every possible aspect of your life.

I believe the best way to generate more time is to use accelerators. Back to the runway of life analogy—while a jet fighter cannot increase the length of a runway, it can use afterburners to massively accelerate and take off in half the distance. Like a jet, you too can use accelerators to massively increase your capacity and achieve more results in a shorter period of time.

Quality education is one type of accelerator. Whether at a top high school, university or night school, or even the school of hard knocks, we can massively increase our capacity in a very short period of time and learn skills from those who have gone before us.

What are the other accelerators that can you use? Try these:

Take the Toughest Job Assignment Possible. This will force you outside your comfort zone and move you to quickly sharpen your skills to be successful. It will also likely bring you the attention of decision-makers and customers. By taking on a big challenge and building new skills, you become more valuable and marketable, leading to a higher income.

Leverage All Resources Available to You. We rarely take a detailed inventory of all available resources, such as our network, special talents, unique relationships, materials that can be converted to cash, and undeveloped potential. Only by detailing what we already have, rather than hoping for something we don't have, can we leverage those resources to accelerate our achievement.

Use Your Imagination. Humans are creatures of habit—when faced with a problem, we try to solve it the same way we have in the past. Use your imagination to look at a problem in a different way. This will help you to solve the problem more quickly. Push yourself to come up with creative solutions, rather than using the same old approach.

Massively Change Your Environment. Several times in my career when I felt I needed a significant boost, I massively changed my environment. This gave me a new perspective, which enabled me to solve a problem or achieve success more quickly. It can be as simple as adding some new people to your network or changing offices, or as dramatic as moving to a new city. A fresh approach opens your mind to new possibilities and lets you accelerate your accomplishments by letting go of past obstacles.

Get Collaborators. With access to social media and an interconnected society, it is easy to find collaborators for nearly anything. If you are feeling stuck or if the pace of your change is too slow, don't try to do it all yourself. Reach out to a group of like-minded people, spread the work around and dramatically accelerate your efforts. Use your time wisely and accelerate massively.

HABIT 16

VISUALIZE YOUR FUTURE SUCCESS

"If you can dream it, you can achieve it." | Zig Ziglar

Vision is the ability to see something that does not yet exist, in a way that is compelling, clear and inspirational. As humans, we often allow ourselves to be limited by our own imagination or shortcomings. Current and past experiences become the framework for our world and can limit our vision of the future.

Like faith, we tend to have vision in abundance when we don't need it, such as when we are progressing forward. We lack vision when we need it the most: when we are stuck. The key is to get into the habit of maintaining a positive vision of the future at all times and to focus on its achievement until your vision becomes a reality.

When I had my epiphany and decided to turn my life around, I was far from my goals. I was unemployed, with no skills, no connections, no capital and no direction. However, I had a vision. My father had given me a book by Maxwell Maltz called *Psycho-Cybernetics* (Psycho-Cybernetics Foundation, 1960), which basically said that your mind cannot tell the difference between an imagined experience and a real one. Therefore, if you hold a vision in your mind of what you want to achieve with enough intensity and conviction, you will start acting as though it has happened. This idea had a tremendous impact on me. After my epiphany and reading this book, I would hold the vision in my mind of what I intended to become. I held it with such intensity that I actually imagined what my office and home would look like, how I would work, and what I would achieve. This vision ultimately became a reality.

How do you visualize your own success? Try the following:

Find or Create a Quiet Place to Visualize Your Future. Maybe it's your office, a quiet room or another favorite place. Even closing your eyes and relaxing in a busy environment helps create the right mood and brings a sense of relaxation and calm that focuses your mind.

Learn to Meditate and Practice Daily. This will get you into the habit of taking some time to remind yourself of what you are focused on achieving, and it will keep you energized for the rest of the day. Meditation is a great way of centering your thoughts so you focus on the critical few, not the trivial many. It lowers emotional tension and is great for reducing stress.

Be Precise in Your Visualization. Imagine exactly what you want to achieve, right down to the look of the environment, and the feeling you will have when you are in your environment. Be very specific. See yourself in that situation and imagine how you will feel.

Don't Hold Back. Since you are only visualizing, there is no need to put limits on what you plan to achieve. Really let your imagination go. Think of a big, compelling and interesting future. Let the creativity of your unconscious mind open and become limitless, helping to expand your horizons by removing preconceived and artificial barriers.

HABIT 17

STAY ON TRACK WITH A DAILY AFFIRMATION

"Winning is not important, but wanting to win is." | Vince Lombardi

Successful advertisers understand the power of repetition. This explains why you frequently hear the same advertisement repeated so often. Advertisers understand that their product or service needs to be kept in the forefront of the consumer's mind, so when the consumer makes a purchasing decision they instinctively think of that product or service. The advertisers' idea is to pound their message into your subconscious mind through repetitive communications, so the recall is instantaneous and emotional, not slow and logical.

You can use this approach to your advantage by creating a commercial with you as the product, by writing a daily affirmation statement describing what you want to achieve, why you want to achieve it, and how you plan to achieve it and by what date. This will help drive your current behaviors and make it happen. Like a product purchase decision that has not happened yet, this future you is a state waiting to happen.

Write a daily affirmation statement, and keep the following key points in mind to make it effective:

Keep It Brief. Aim for less than 100 words, so it can be read in about one minute. This will force you to be succinct.

Use Affirmative Words. Write it with phrases like "I will…" and "I am…" so you are speaking as if it will happen—so it does happen.

Include Results. Describe the results or future state you intend to achieve, in concrete, numerical and clear terms.

Articulate Key Actions. Talk about what actions you will take to achieve your results, including what you will and will not do. Decide what you intend to give up to make it happen.

Incorporate Emotion. Use strong language that will elicit a deep, powerful and positive emotion to motivate and encourage you.

Commit. Sign it and read it daily, or several times a day. Keep it nearby so you can access it readily and read it when you have a moment or need a boost.

HABIT 18

IMPLEMENT THE PLAN-DO-CHECK-ACT SYSTEM

"Discipline yourself and others won't need to." | Coach John Wooden

Everybody needs a plan! Coaches have a game plan, pilots have a flight plan, investors have an investment plan and architects create a building plan—the list goes on. Nothing of great substance happens without a plan. Of course, plans are not worth the paper they are written on if they are not followed by actions.

Losers plan, plan and plan some more. Winners plan for success, do something, check the results, act again to make the plan better, and then repeat the whole cycle. *Plan-Do-Check-Act.*

The first time I came across this concept was when I was learning statistical process control (SPC) as a young engineer with the Ford Motor Company. At the time, Ford was embracing the teachings of Edward Deming and instructing every employee on the fundamentals of statistical measure and process improvement. We quickly implemented statistical analysis on key manufacturing processes to compare the actual process performance with the planned performance. Using this technique, we quickly discovered any deviation from the plan and took the necessary steps to understand the problem, correct it and improve the process. This rapid *Plan, Do, Check, Act* feedback struck me intensely. I realized that, if this could work so effectively at a small level, surely it could work on a big level.

In subsequent companies, I used this concept at a strategic level. I would ensure a strategic plan was in place; execute the plan with the right level of detail, commitment and infrastructure to do a great job; measure the results; and then modify accordingly. If it works for some of the biggest companies in the world, then it can work for you.

When planning for a project, do the following:

Plan: Make a clear, concise and action-oriented plan of what you intend to achieve, including specific goals, measures and resources, and the steps necessary to achieve success.

Do: Execute the plan immediately, ensuring you have the right resources in place, and the coordination of activity, incentives, alignment and accountability. Focus and play to win.

Check: Measure the results of your action in a clear, accurate and timely manner, and communicate those results with all who need to know.

Act: Determine how your results vary from the plan, and then take the actions necessary to make improvements based on this deviation.

This simple *Plan-Do-Check-Act* routine can be applied to all types of organizations, and even at a personal level, in order to focus actions and improve results.

ACTIONS FOR TRACTION

What is your definite purpose?

_____

_____

_____

Write the three top goals you plan to accomplish this year.

_____

_____

_____

Name three collaborators who want you to achieve your three goals.

_____

_____

_____

What is a career accelerator, and how can you use one now?

_____

_____

_____

CHAPTER 4

OVERCOMING OBSTACLES

"Twenty years from now you will be more disappointed by
the things that you didn't do than by the ones you did do,
so throw off the bowlines, sail away from safe harbor, and
catch the trade winds in your sails." | Mark Twain

MY STORY: STARTING OFF BROKE

With my acceptance to Lakehead University in hand, all I needed
to do now was to drive from Vancouver to Northern Ontario, take
a two-month preparatory calculus course as the requirement of
acceptance into the full engineering program, complete two years
of engineering school, and do it with none of my own money! I had
already spent all of my savings that I had set aside to get through
BCIT. Now I took out a student loan to finish my degree.

I needed transportation to get from Vancouver, British Columbia,
to Thunder Bay, Ontario, a distance of about 1,900 miles. I bought
a 1976 Plymouth Volare Sedan at a local surplus vehicle auction by
putting in 'stink bids' of $55 on 30 cars simultaneously, thinking
there was the possibility that one car may not get any bids. I was right

and bought a car for $55. I then purchased four new tires, a roof rack and a fire extinguisher, and proceeded to drive across Canada on the July 1st (Canada Day) long weekend of 1984.

I literally had no money. While I had been approved for the student loan, the loan had yet to come in and I only had the cash that I had saved up from working for a few weeks after finishing BCIT. I drove across the country with all of my worldly possessions in my car. It took me three days to drive across Canada; I slept in my car for two nights, arriving in Northern Ontario on the third day. A low engine oil light had been flashing on and off throughout the whole trip and periodically I would stop and top up the engine oil. There must have been a leak in the engine because the warning light was coming on with increasing frequency. (What do you expect for $55?)

As I approached Thunder Bay, I passed a little town called Upsala and was now only about 90 miles from Thunder Bay. I knew that I was nearly there, but the oil light continued to flash on and off. As I got closer, the day got hotter and the oil pressure got lower. Thinking that I was close enough and I didn't have to put any more oil in the car, I gunned it toward Thunder Bay, which was my last thought before I heard a terrific noise as the engine seized and the car rolled to a silent stop. Leaving my car with all my possessions on the side of the road, I hitchhiked back to Upsala and had my car towed back to the town. I managed to negotiate the sale of the car to the local garage for what I had put into it—the $55 plus the cost of the four tires, roof rack and fire extinguisher. I settled for cash, walked to the side of the road with only my valuables in an overnight bag, and hitchhiked into Thunder Bay.

When I got to Thunder Bay, a friend agreed to drive me back out to Upsala to pick up the remainder of my possessions (which I had to leave at the gas station because I couldn't take everything with me) and that is how I arrived in Thunder Bay, Ontario. At this point, I was still on my mission to achieve the first of my five major goals and nothing was going to stop me. There was now nothing further to prevent me from achieving what I knew was important in my life, and I embarked on a program of intensive study in electrical engineering at Lakehead University. With very remedial math skills and a poor academic track record, and far away from family and friends, I was 100% on my own.

I was well into the Lakehead program and in my final year when the cash from my first loan eventually ran out. One night, while studying for yet another calculus test, I was up until almost midnight feeling sluggish and wanted to prop myself up with some coffee. I went to my desk to find the 25 cents needed to buy a cup of coffee from the shop in the basement of the dorm hall (coffee was cheap back then). I searched through my belongings on my desk and could find nothing. I could not find any cash, any change—<u>nothing</u>. I looked in my pencil cup where I normally kept all my change and found 17 cents. I didn't even have enough money for a cup of coffee. I was completely and utterly broke for the first time in my life. In fact, I was worth more dead than alive at this point because, in addition to having no cash, I had a $30,000 student loan that I had already borrowed to get me to this point. I went to bed without the coffee.

The next day, I went to student services at the university administration, as I had heard that they granted emergency student loans. I was embarrassed but asked for an emergency loan to get me through a few days while I waited for the last payment from my student loan to come through. The woman opened the drawer, took out five $20 bills and handed them to me. That $100 kept me going until the final payment of my loan came through.

I worked hard to finish the program and successfully graduated. After that entire experience, I thought to myself, "I will never ever be without money again. For the rest of my life, I am never going through that experience again. I will never be broke again!"

HABIT 19

FOCUS ON YOUR STRENGTHS, BUT KNOW YOUR WEAKNESSES

"You can journey to the ends of the earth in search of success, but if you're lucky, you will discover happiness in your own backyard." | Russell H. Conwell

How many times in your career have you heard that you should focus on your weaknesses, or that we all have weaknesses we must work to overcome? I don't buy it. I think we should get into the habit of focusing on our strengths. By focusing on our weaknesses, we are reminding ourselves of the aspects of our life where we are least capable, rather than the most. By focusing on our strengths, we concentrate on reinforcing the capabilities we already have, which saves us the time and energy necessary to build new skills.

Each of us has a unique set of natural talents and learned skills, and sometimes we underestimate the power of these abilities. Too often, we look to others who seem to have more abilities or advantages than we do, without recognizing the significance of our own. I urge you to focus on your individual strengths. While you should not ignore your weaknesses, you should make them a smaller priority and focus most of your energy on your strengths.

Here's what I suggest specifically:

Take the Time to Understand Your Strengths. Go through an assessment. Write them down. Be quite detailed. Prioritize them from beginning to end and understand exactly why you believe those are your strengths.

Focus on What You Can Do Now. How are your particular strengths or abilities unique in your industry or in the market sector you are focused on? How can you leverage them to create value?

Develop Your Strengths Further. Just having strengths and focusing on using them is not enough. Like building muscle, which needs to be worked each day, strengths need to be developed further. Improve your skills through education and use.

Remind Yourself Daily. Add them to your daily affirmation statement to remind yourself regularly. By focusing on your strengths over time, you will move to an area where you have greater capability, giving you more strength and success.

Ignore the Naysayers. Many people become obsessively concerned with correcting weaknesses (especially other people's weaknesses), even if they are relatively minor. Respectfully ignore these people, particularly if you don't feel they have your best interests in mind, or the credibility and merit to justify their approach. Stay focused on what you do best!

HABIT 20

ACT AS IF YOU WILL SUCCEED

"Whatever you are, be a good one." | Abraham Lincoln

Finding yourself in a situation where you are trying something for the first time is progress. You should frequently be in situations where you are learning something new and finding it difficult. This is the only way we grow and progress. We are often dropped into uncertain situations through a change in employment or family circumstances, and we have to take on a new role.

The best way to handle these types of situations is to act as if you know what to do, or, to fake it until you make it. By acting as if you know what to do, you put yourself in a position of creating momentum. Instead of becoming paralyzed, you start to move forward. You will often find that you have previously unrecognized skills or capabilities that are helpful in this situation. Once you start acting, you find yourself moving forward and making progress.

The key is to do something, keep doing it and not overthink it. Move forward as best you can with the resources in front of you. By projecting confidence and the impression that you know what you are doing, you will find that people around you are more receptive and supportive. If you overanalyze the situation, you will find many reasons not to proceed, instead of making progress. These are opportunities to develop, build capability and show courage.

If you are in an unfamiliar situation or feel anxious, yet want to act successfully, I suggest the following:

Control Your Breathing. When we get anxious we start to breathe more rapidly, which decreases the amount of carbon dioxide in our blood stream. If it becomes excessive, it can lead to dizziness, dry mouth and other symptoms. If nervous, concentrate on breathing slowly and deeply. This will cause you to relax and create a greater sense of control and confidence.

Simply Smile. Many people tend to mirror behavior. By smiling, you are broadcasting to those around you that you are approachable, in control and relaxed in a situation. Don't grin like a Cheshire cat, just smile in a relaxed and friendly way.

Let the Small Things Go. We all make small faux pas like calling someone by the wrong name or making other minor social mistakes. If that happens to you, move on as quickly as possible and put it out of your mind. Practice saying "Oh well." with a shrug of your shoulders or "So what? Next!" and move on.

Dominate Your Space. Internal confidence can be generated by expanding your external space. If we shrink space physically, we tend to shrink mentally. Open up. Walk into a room like you own the place and your confidence will rise.

HABIT 21

GET HOPE AND INSPIRATION FROM YOUR PAST SUCCESSES

"We become what we think about." | Earl Nightingale

There have been countless times in my career when the situation did not look great. In fact, it looked utterly hopeless. What I did in these situations was generate hope that the situation would improve while dealing with the practical reality facing me. I have found over the years that the following technique worked particularly well for me: *I reminded myself of my past successes and the challenges that I overcame.*

Now, I keep a list of all the things I am most proud of since the beginning of my career. It includes about 30 of my most significant life accomplishments, such as graduating from university, getting my first job, buying my first house, etc. I read the list when I hit a rough patch or I am not quite sure what the next steps are, and it gives me hope that my current situation will improve.

In addition to giving me hope, this list shows me how patterns developed over my lifetime. I can see that, over time, while there have been ups and downs, my trajectory has been to improve. This pattern often gives me hope, particularly if I am mired in a short-term, day-by-day problem and I start to lose perspective of the long term. It always gives me hope!

While these improvements don't manifest themselves every single day, I know that they are coming just over the horizon. Call it faith, or unfounded optimism, but for a goal-oriented person like me, I know for sure that the future gets brighter. Always has, always will!

If you find yourself feeling hopeless about your situation, make your own list. Don't overthink it, just jot down a list of those accomplishments of which you are most proud. This is important, since it is your list and you need to remind yourself of what worked for you, not society's expectation of you.

Go back early into your life, to young adulthood or even childhood. There are many defining experiences in the early part of our lives that are often underestimated. Don't dwell on them; write them down if they resonate with you. If you are a young person starting your career, do not be reluctant to include your early accomplishments such as academic performance, sports and artistic accomplishments— anything that enabled you to overcome an obstacle.

Once the list is complete, draw upon your experiences to spot the trends. Look for those times in your career where you made significant progress and seek to understand why.

If you are facing an obstacle, go back to the list and find a time where you faced a similar obstacle, and then look at all the accomplishments that immediately followed it. This will give you a renewed sense of hope that your situation will get better and that brighter days are ahead.

HABIT 22

UNDERSTAND THE RISKS AND MITIGATE THEM

"Experience is a truer guide than the words of others." | Leonardo da Vinci

There is no such thing as risk-free living, but if you follow the principles of *The 1% Solution*, you can reduce risk and improve your probability of success.

If you are about to embark on a certain project or a venture, list all the significant risks associated with that project. For most projects, whether it is professional or personal, there are usually about five to 10 risks in the medium-to-significant range, with only one or two being the most significant risks.

Now, prioritize the list, and for each risk write a simple statement or action on how to reduce it. Ask yourself what you can do to mitigate the probability of each risk occurring. You will quickly find that most of the risks are fairly minor to begin with, and the most significant risks can be reduced in some way. The process itself will help you determine whether it is worth pursuing the project, as often a project initially looks more daunting, only to reveal itself as more manageable when you break the risks into bite-sized pieces.

If you're embarking on something more significant, such as a new business, this can be a fairly rigorous process and it should be worked into your business plan or your growth plan.

Nothing is risk-free, and life's biggest rewards often go to those taking some of the biggest risks, or what seem like risks. The point of this approach is to be methodical and not to take unnecessary or reckless risks that you could have reduced with some thought and planning.

I find that many seemingly small projects go poorly when risks stack up and cause a massive failure.

As Benjamin Franklin said,

> *"For want of a nail the shoe was lost; for want of a shoe the horse was lost; and for want of a horse the rider was lost; being overtaken and slain by the enemy, all for want of care about a horse-shoe nail."*

Be smart—do not put yourself, your family and your capital at unnecessary risk. This process will help you evaluate whether or not you want to move forward with a project, and if you do, you will be better prepared and have a higher probability of success.

HABIT 23

PROGRESS BY CHOOSING THE NEXT BEST ALTERNATIVE

"If you hear a voice within you say 'you cannot paint,' then by all means paint and that voice will be silenced." | Vincent van Gogh

Excellence is always the long-term goal. Unfortunately, some people get bogged down in the details while seeking excellence; they lose focus, excellence fades and they hit a dead end. This causes them to freeze or become overly inhibited by the fear of making a mistake. They end up doing nothing and the initiative stalls.

I have learned over the years that circumstances are never perfect, so you have to work with what is immediately in front of you. A big part of building something important is constantly making decisions using the best information available. These decisions can and must be made. *Decide, Act, Learn, Repeat!*

Resist the temptation to procrastinate, and put all fear of making a wrong decision out of your mind. Instead, when you are prevented from taking the ideal course of action, progress by choosing the next best alternative and act immediately.

Why does this approach work?

- Deciding on the next best alternative creates traction and momentum, and immediately improves on the status quo.

- It reinforces your ability to make a decision, which will ultimately move you forward.

- While the next best alternative is not the final outcome, it creates a different perspective. This may enable you to see the problem in a new light and generate new creative ideas and possible solutions.

- You reduce your risks by making many small decisions. If your decision is a poor one, your failure is small and limited.

- Choosing the next best alternative builds your action muscle. The human condition is about progress, innovation and fulfillment of potential, and action is one of the best ways to make this happen.

How to choose the next best alternative:

1. When faced with a difficult decision, immediately determine two or three short-term actions you can take.

2. Quickly consider the pros and cons of each action, but focus mostly on which option moves you closer to your long-term goal.

3. Pick one option and execute immediately.

4. Don't second-guess yourself. Put all self-doubt out of your mind.

5. Repeat whenever you are faced with a similar situation.

The key is to move beyond the fear and paralysis that can engulf you by taking a small step forward. Don't lose sight of the big picture, which is to ultimately achieve excellence.

HABIT 24

LEARN FROM EVERY FAILURE

*"Life is 10% what happens to me
and 90% of how I react to it."* | Charles Swindoll

Failure can be a good thing if you take it as an opportunity to learn and "start again more intelligently," as Henry Ford said. No one has a consistent track record of success without ever experiencing failure. In fact, if you study the lives of great people, you find they experienced significant, repeated and consistent failure, particularly early in their careers, before success was ultimately achieved.

You will also find, by studying the lives of these successful people, that each failure produced the fruit of future success.

Abraham Lincoln famously failed many times, including one failed business, one lost sweetheart and seven losses for political office. However, he went on to win more often than he failed, and eventually became the President of the United States.

Henry Ford started as a machinist and went bankrupt twice before finally successfully launching the Ford Motor Company.

Steve Jobs was fired from Apple, the company he co-founded, only to be rehired, leading the company to incredible success.

Walt Disney was a high school dropout who was once fired for 'not being creative enough.' He went on to launch and build one of the greatest entertainment companies in the world.

Even the best and the brightest have failed at one point but bounced back. If they can do it, so can you!

Once you have failed, strive to learn why and what to do differently next time. If you fail and then do the same thing without learning, you will never achieve success, as you haven't learned any lessons from the failure.

Be objective and realistic about failure. Do not spend hours dwelling on it; instead, examine it and see what you can learn from it. Apply your new knowledge to your next endeavor, and you will find that, over time, your rate of failure will go down, and the magnitude of those failures will likely decrease.

HABIT 25

FIND THE PATH FROM TRUSTED ADVISERS AND MENTORS

"Young people need models,
not critics." | Coach John Wooden

I have always found it interesting that we try to do everything ourselves. There is not enough time in our short lives to do all the things that are necessary to achieve our goals. There are people who have gone before us who have learned much more than we have. Many of these people are more than happy to share their experiences, helping us become better people.

How do you seek the guidance of trusted advisers and mentors?

Target the Right Kind of Mentor. A mentor is someone who works with you to help leverage your core strengths, and who has done what you want to do. A trusted adviser is somebody who works with you on the tactical items. If you are seeking a mentor, be selective. This person is not necessarily the most popular or prominent person in the community, but somebody that you feel has the skills and abilities to help you grow. This may be somebody who has chosen a career similar to what you want to do and has done it successfully.

Connect and Create Value. Write a letter, make a phone call or connect through a mutual contact. Find a way to create value and a mutually beneficial relationship. For instance, in exchange for mentorship and support over time, you may be able to give him or her insight into your industry, new connections that may be important, or even support a cause that he or she cares about.

Be Very Respectful of Your Mentor's Time. Meet only a few times a year and keep it brief (an hour for lunch or breakfast). During that time, ask very specific questions that will help you grow. Come prepared. Take his or her advice seriously. If you decide not to act on the advice, be clear as to why you are not acting on it and let the mentor know.

Become a Mentor Yourself. By taking the time to mentor another person, you will not only give back but will improve your own skills and get a better appreciation for what your mentor feels. This reciprocity will help you get more out of both relationships.

Develop these types of relationships over time and learn from successful people. These people will make the way easier for you, accelerate your progress, and help you overcome fear and obstacles.

HABIT 26

COURSE-CORRECT OVER TIME AS CIRCUMSTANCES CHANGE

*"You can never cross the ocean until you have the courage
to lose sight of the shore."* | Christopher Columbus

Global trends in technology, economics and demographics are changing rapidly; as circumstances change, so should you.

Most people think that Darwin came up with the term 'survival of the fittest,' but this is incorrect. In fact, his theory of evolution is based on adaptability over long periods of time, not fitness at a point in time. The ability to adapt is necessary to achieve the important things in your life as circumstances evolve.

The path to success is never direct or a straight line. It's more like climbing a lattice, not a ladder. Sometimes it's up, sometimes down, and often sideways. As you find yourself deviating from that path, you course-correct back to your long-term objective. Those course corrections are small tactical things that you need to do throughout the day, week or month. Another analogy would be an airplane flying across the ocean. While pilots steer toward the final destination, they are actually making thousands of minute course corrections throughout the flight.

Here is how to course-correct over time:

Stay Focused on Your Objective. Don't keep changing your long-term goal, as this will cause you to course-correct to two or three different destinations, rather than sticking with a single one.

Review Your Activities Weekly. Find out what worked, what didn't and what you need to change for the following week. Keep your learning cycle time short.

Have the Courage to Make Changes When Necessary. If you find that something is not working, recognize that it is time to make a change. Perhaps you are trying to start a business in an unsuitable area, or an employee you hired is not working out. People ask me how much effort I put into something before I either make a change or admit that it did not work out. There is no easy answer. It is always a judgment call, and up to the individual person to decide when he or she thinks it is enough. However, we usually have a tendency to quit too soon.

Never Quit. Before you think of quitting, see if there is some small adjustment you can make to course-correct. This little change may be the step necessary to get back on track and move aggressively toward your goals. Take a pause before you think of quitting. Gather up your strengths and start again.

ACTIONS FOR TRACTION

Make a list of your strengths and post it so it can be read daily.

_____

_____

_____

Describe one episode of your peak performance and what caused it to happen.

_____

_____

_____

List the risks associated with an upcoming project, and the actions you can take to mitigate those risks.

_____

_____

_____

Who would be a great mentor for you and why? What can you offer him or her in return?

_____

_____

_____

CHAPTER 5

BUILDING A CAREER

"Pray as though everything depended on God. Work as though everything depended on you." | Saint Augustine

MY STORY: MY FIRST REAL JOB

My working career began shortly after my studies finished. After four grueling years, I finally finished my engineering degree and decided to drive back from Thunder Bay to Vancouver. I drove with a classmate in his Toyota pickup truck, with our possessions overloaded in the back; we left within four hours of finishing my last final exam.

We drove through an ice storm in Kenora, just east of Winnipeg, and then drove across the Prairies all night, arriving in British Columbia the next day. We continued through the Rockies to the town of Ashcroft, where my friend lived. He dropped me off at the Greyhound bus terminal so that I could take the bus home in the morning.

I arrived in Vancouver on the morning of May 2, 1986, which happened to be my birthday and the opening day of the Expo 86

World Fair. I vividly remember my father picking me up at the bus depot and bringing me home, where my mother had laid out a beautiful breakfast. There was nothing more pleasurable than sitting in that kitchen enjoying the first home-cooked meal I had had in a long time, as the sun poured through the window on that early May morning.

I was fortunate to experience Expo 86, as my parents had purchased a season's pass for me as a gift for finishing my engineering program. However, September of 1986 soon came and, as anybody who has spent much time in Vancouver knows, when the summer ends, the rain typically starts.

It was time for me to start building my career. I knew I had some market-ready skills, but I was in the wrong market, so I decided to go where the action was—Toronto. I went down to the travel agent and asked for a one-way ticket to Toronto. I remember that she asked, "Are you sure you want a <u>one-way</u> ticket to Toronto? Nobody buys a <u>one-way</u> ticket to Toronto. Everybody buys a return ticket!"

I bought the one-way ticket on a Monday and by Friday of that week, I was in Toronto. I stayed with a friend for a couple of weeks and immediately started my job search. I had the presence of mind to know that I needed to move quickly, since I felt that I had finished my education later than most, at age 25, and needed to make up for lost time.

Within a week of arriving, while scouring the career section of the *Toronto Star*, I saw a job with the Ford Electronics Manufacturing Corporation in Markham, Ontario. I called them up, was given an interview, was offered the job and accepted it immediately. The position was a Production Supervisor in a large, high-volume, advanced electronics manufacturing facility. I knew little about manufacturing, less about electronics and nothing about being a

Production Supervisor. However, they saw something in me and gave me a chance. They offered me the midnight shift, and soon afterward I was on my way to my first shift on a Sunday night at 11 pm.

Working for a big international company in an environment where there was a tremendous amount of opportunity to learn was an incredible experience. I moved from role to role in order to pick up new skills. I relished the experience and decided that this was what I needed to do to move fast and to make up for lost time (and money). One of the most important things I did was give myself a challenge of getting a new role within the company every 18 months so that I could ramp up my skills quickly. I did this by promoting my talent, getting things done, taking on the hardest jobs I could find and doing them to the best of my abilities. I also worked hard at developing my leadership skills by taking every opportunity for training and learning, such as public speaking at Toastmasters. Finally, I always focused on solving real problems and adding significant value, so I was known as a doer, not simply a thinker. I ended up getting a new role about every 12 months and was promoted twice in the five-year period I was there.

I immersed myself in difficult and challenging roles, so the skills and learning came fast. I did not want anything easy; I wanted everything difficult, with lots of obstacles, because I knew that I was building my career and that what I learned in the early first few years would separate me from the crowd. I knew I had a lot of competition, from very capable men and women my age. I worked hard and built my skills fast in my five years at Ford, and my career was launched.

HABIT 27

DO WORK YOU ENJOY AND FOLLOW THE MONEY

"The two most important days in your life are the day you were born and the day you find out why." | Mark Twain

We have a relatively short amount of time in our lives to amass the wealth necessary to provide for ourselves, our families, and a comfortable life in old age. Many trials and difficulties face us as we accumulate wealth, and many seem insurmountable. With conventional, rational, linear thinking, they are insurmountable, since a rational person would not endure such hardship without quitting, particularly over a long period of time. It takes something else. It takes an unconventional and unreasonable approach in order to break away from average to achieve something exceptional. It takes supernatural faith.

You must have the skills necessary to create value in the marketplace, and adapt these skills to survive market changes. **The key is to do some kind of work you enjoy _and_ something you know _and_ follow the money.** It is not sufficient to just follow your passion without any regard to developing the skills necessary to create value. Find the area where your enjoyment and knowledge intersect, so you can create value in the marketplace while following the money. It is still work, but will not feel like it.

This approach is very dependent on your stage of life. When starting your career, you haven't figured out what you enjoy or developed any marketable skills. Often, young people take the first job that comes along, which takes them in a specific direction whether they like it or not. If you are young, I recommend pursuing areas of interest early in your career while building transferable skills (such as leadership, communications and critical thinking) that you can take from job to job, until you do find the role you enjoy. Don't forget to follow the money.

At the midpoint of your career, you should be doing what you enjoy, should have marketable skills and should be making good money. If you want to make a career transition, do not quit your current job until you have found something else better. The subsequent financial and emotional turmoil of being unemployed is not worth it. Start a business on the side, or build skills slowly and then make a transition. *Keep moving toward the intersection of what you know and enjoy, and what makes money.*

If you are near the end of your career, you will likely be at the point of maximum skill level, based on your many years of working, and can aggressively move toward areas of personal fulfillment. Don't think about retiring, only repositioning. Constantly evaluate your career position and move toward that satisfying and valuable intersection of your knowledge, skills and money. Do it methodically and you may find yourself there more quickly than you thought.

Draw a Venn diagram (three overlapping circles) to best understand how these worlds can work together. In one circle, make a list of all the things you enjoy doing, and in the second circle, make a list of all the things that you are good at doing, in the third, make a list of how money can be made. At the intersection of the three circles, write down the items that appear in all three circles. This is where you need to start your search for a meaningful career.

While it will not happen overnight, knowing and pursuing that sweet spot will bring you much closer to ultimately finding the dream career that will give you the highest probability of future success.

HABIT 28

CREATE A UNIQUE, VALUABLE AND ENDURING SKILL SET

"Strive not to be a success, but rather to be of value." | Albert Einstein

Progress has always been achieved as the result of the specialization and division of labor. We succeed each day because we focus on a single task that creates value in the marketplace and generates the income we need to acquire necessities of life (food, energy, shelter, transportation), which were produced as a result of the specialization of others. It's specialization that creates value. The more valuable your specialization, the higher you will be compensated.

Specializations change over time as market conditions, technology and other factors evolve. For instance, we have moved from the Industrial Age to the Digital Age and then to the Information Age very quickly. These changes have massively displaced people who did not upgrade their skills. As we move into the Innovation Age, this displacement will be repeated. Therefore, it becomes a matter of survival to create skills that endure over time. Keep a mindset of continuous personal improvement so you can transform your skills over your lifetime.

Your skill set should be **valuable**, since the more the market values your skill set, the greater the demand for your services, and the higher your compensation, which enables you to reinvest in yourself and to make yourself more valuable as the cycle repeats.

Your skill set should be **unique**. We live in a highly globalized world where competition has moved from local to global, from physical to online, from generalist to specialist. Becoming exceptional at a niche skill will enable you to sell to the broader global market, not only your local market. It will also make you an expert and build a strong personal brand.

Your skill set should be **enduring**, particularly in this age of significant technological, demographic and economic change. Focus on a skill set that can withstand the changes of time. For instance, people, financial and leadership skills are base skills that will serve you well, no matter how the world changes.

Here is how to create a unique, valuable and enduring skill set:

1. Stick with one occupation or sector for an extended period of time, so you can develop deep expertise in that area.

2. Pick a trend that is rising, like a wave, and is multiple decades long (e.g., genetics). Avoid industries in decline.

3. Strive to be the best in your sector, no matter what it may be. Eventually you will get noticed.

4. Constantly seek to improve all levels of your personal and professional development. Never stagnate.

5. Invest heavily in yourself through taking courses, seminars, reading quality books, and any other skill upgrades.

6. Get external, qualified, third-party assessments of your strengths and weaknesses. Be brutally honest with yourself.

7. Make transferable skills a priority, particularly in the areas of leadership, communications, time management, finance, public speaking and interpersonal skills.

HABIT 29

THINK IN TERMS OF DECADES, NOT YEARS

"Life shrinks or expands in proportion to one's courage." | *Anaïs Nin*

Given the distractions and difficulties of daily living, we often get into the habit of thinking tactically, rather than strategically. While the momentum and importance of daily actions are critical to the achievement of our goals, periodically we need to take the long view.

A few years ago, I walked a section of the ancient pilgrimage path of the Camino de Santiago in Spain and averaged about 19 miles of walking per day. While the majority of my time was spent viewing the path immediately in front of me, periodically I would glance up and view the distant mountaintops where I was heading. This glimpse of a distant peak gave me a newfound energy to move forward, and encouragement that the individual steps would amount to something bigger.

We often vastly overestimate what we can achieve in a short period of time (such as a year), and underestimate what we can achieve in a long period of time (such as a lifetime). This can hamper our own progress, and like my walk on the Camino de Santiago, can risk moving our perspective only to the short term.

Careers, families, health and financial freedom are achieved over lengthy periods and result in consistent effort and persistence in overcoming regular obstacles, with little short-term incentive or reward. If we think long-term, to understand better where we are going and why we are going there, our work becomes more meaningful and the burden lightens.

Here are the best ways I have found to maintain a long-term perspective:

Create a mission statement and read it at least once per day. It should remind you why you are doing what you do, and inspire you to action.

Rewrite your goals every morning to remind yourself what you are working toward.

At the end of the day, write down a significant accomplishment from that day, particularly as it relates to your long-term goals and the habits you need to develop.

Focus on completing strategic actions (important and valuable) and minimize the tactical (urgent but not important).

HABIT 30

CREATE CAREER CRITICAL MASS

"Whatever you can do, or dream you can,
begin it. Boldness has genius, power, and
magic in it." | Johann Wolfgang von Goethe

Have you ever seen a seriously big bonfire? It burns with incredible intensity, and any wood that gets thrown into it is consumed fast. It keeps burning long after the fuel supply ends, and the embers can ignite quickly long after the flames are gone. It is an impressive sight.

Great careers are like an enormous bonfire. You start with an idea (build), you add energy (fuel), the right environment (oxygen) and action (spark), and you get ignition. The more energy you add, the longer and more brightly it burns. Once the fire is burning, it creates tremendous heat and continues to burn for a long time, only requiring a steady supply of fuel. It has achieved critical mass.

Building critical mass is very important since it gives you a safety margin, i.e., the ability to withstand shocks and to persevere over a long period of time. Inevitably, we will all face shocks to our plans, and without a strong critical mass, a small shock to your system may become fatal.

You can turn your career from a campfire to a bonfire and achieve critical mass by ramping up your energy, creating a good environment, and taking persistent action. The career equivalents for energy are: skills, knowledge, experiences, resources and mindset. The right environment is made up of your colleagues, network, partner, family. Finally, you need the spark of action. Not occasional halfhearted action, but massive, unrelenting, 100% commitment action.

Once you have achieved career critical mass, you will be able to burn more brightly, earn more and overcome the occasional setback. Critical mass provides a pool of stored energy that can be released when necessary, is hardly dampened, and can be flared up upon demand with the addition of a modest amount of fuel.

To achieve career critical mass, do the following:

Go All in All the Time. Fully commit yourself to building skills, experiences and contacts, particularly early in your career. Never take your foot off the accelerator.

Stay Connected with Your Network. This will exert a tremendous influence on building the critical mass necessary to help maintain it during dry spells.

Stay Authentic. Be yourself and stick to your core values, even if they are out of favor. Good values triumph in the end.

Put Setbacks in Perspective. Nothing great is achieved without setbacks. Keep the long-term view in perspective and put setbacks behind you fast.

Reframe Failure. Any failure is the result of an action, and its cause and effect. Focus on understanding what was wrong with the action, and fix it.

HABIT 31

BE THE BEST AND DOMINATE YOUR SECTOR

"We must believe that we are gifted for something and that this thing, at whatever cost, must be attained." | Marie Curie

If you look at the world's most successful business leaders, athletes, performers or musicians, they have one thing in common—they dominate their sector! Amazon doesn't plan to just compete or be number two in their space, so why should you? At his peak, Tiger Woods wiped the ground with his competition in order to stay on top. Google wants to own the Information Age, not just compete in it.

Unfortunately, many people take an 'average is good enough' approach to their work and careers. They may be inhibited and are reluctant to stand out from the crowd, or perhaps they are fearful of being separated from their peers by success, or maybe they never had an exceptional role model. For whatever reason, the average is good enough for many people.

In the long run, this mindset will hurt them, as the world's technology, demographics and economy are changing rapidly. The internet has created a competitive global economy, millennials are smart and motivated to work hard, and the middle class is being squeezed down by taxation, regulation and inflation.

Keep these points in mind daily to help you be the best:

Plan to Dominate Your Sector. Even if you shoot for the best but fall short, you will be much further ahead than if you plan to be average and achieve it.

Prepare for Hardship. The earliest homesteaders faced the roughest conditions, but also settled the best lands. Those who came later had an easier time but were left with the rocky soil.

Set Massive Goals. Make your goals bigger than anything you have ever conceived before, and much bigger than those around you. Shoot for the stars.

Become an Expert in Your Field. Attaining expert status in your field will ultimately enable you to dominate the competition and create long-term value for your employer, clients and customers.

Build a Reputation as the Go-to Person. To dominate market position means that you are, without any doubt, the go-to person for your particular sector. Your reputation means that you consistently deliver value well above and beyond your competition.

HABIT 32

NEVER LOSE MOMENTUM

*"Never give in, never give in,
never, never, never!"* | Winston Churchill

Many of the great truths of life are captured in simple sayings, and "A rolling stone gathers no moss" is one of them. It illustrates the importance of always maintaining full momentum in all of your activities in order to avoid becoming stagnant. Momentum is energy carried forward over obstacles and difficulties. It maintains our inertia, with only the small additional amount of energy in order to keep things moving forward. For instance, a flywheel (a heavy spinning disk) takes a tremendous amount of energy to start moving, but only takes a small amount of energy to keep moving.

Your career is like a flywheel. Once you have it up and running, it is important to keep it going. Don't get sidetracked, lose focus or take too much time off; you risk dissipating all the energy you have created over your lifetime.

Career momentum gives you courage and confidence. When your colleagues and associates know you never stop, it becomes part of your personal brand. It also gives you personal confidence, knowing that if you do hit a rough spot or an obstacle, the energy you have put into your career so far may be sufficient to keep it going. With the addition of further energy, it will be enough to get you over any obstacle.

Here are the actions you need to take in order to maintain career momentum:

Remind Yourself that Careers Are Built Over a Lifetime. Pay attention to the amount of energy you need to put into your own career in order to get the lift you need to sustain you over time.

Avoid Taking a Significant Amount of Time Off or Deviating Dramatically from Your Career Goals. This will slow your momentum, and your growth will stagnate. It is better to transition, rather than stop and restart.

Focus on Continuous Improvement and Renewal. Constantly think about adding new skills, taking new seminars, reading new materials, and meeting new people.

Avoid Proximity with People Who Are Coasting or in a Rut. If it is a friend or a colleague who needs a hand, that's no problem, but stay away from business interactions with these people, as they are losing momentum.

Take Dramatic, Swift and Bold Action if your career is starting to lag. This will put the energy back into your career, reverse the decline and ensure you accelerate in the right direction.

ACTIONS FOR TRACTION

What poor habits are holding you back in your career or job?

_____

_____

_____

What is the one new skill you need to develop that is absolutely necessary for your long-term career success?

_____

_____

_____

Who can collaborate with you in building your career and why?

_____

_____

_____

From a job perspective, what worked best for you this week and how do you do more of it?

_____

_____

_____

CHAPTER 6
MANAGING TIME WELL

"It's not the years in your life that counts. It's the life in your years." | Abraham Lincoln

MY STORY: THE FAST TRACK MBA

After the night of my epiphany in my early 20s, which launched me on a journey of self-improvement and progress, I started treating time like the precious and limited resource it truly is. The epiphany spurred me to action and motivated me to finish my formal education and start building a career, but I still felt hungry for more.

Being a late career bloomer, I decided that while I had a secure job with a good company, it was time to build the business and leadership skills that could help me reach my wealth and career aspirations more quickly. I thought getting an MBA would be a great complement to an electrical engineering degree, and help build the business and leadership skills I was missing.

I was living in downtown Toronto and was fortunate to be near one of the best business schools in Canada: the University of Toronto, Faculty of Management (now Rotman School of Management). I could not give up two years of full-time income, so I decided to apply for the part-time program, so I could work during the day, and study during the evenings and weekends.

I lived only a few blocks away from campus and knew that I would be in Toronto for a number of years. I was newly married, without any children, and living in a studio apartment with my wife, so it was a perfect time to apply. All I needed to do was work, study and sleep in order to get it finished (which is exactly what I did). I knew I would have to advance my career not only at Ford, but well into the future if I was to achieve my major goals, and I saw an MBA as the way to make that happen.

The problem was that I had virtually no time to spare. I was working substantially more than full-time at work (since I was paid to work overtime and therefore I did), I commuted at least an hour each day, and I was regularly away on business trips. I decided to go for it anyways and use my weekends to study for the Graduate Management Admission Test (GMAT), which took one year of intensive preparation.

The GMAT was one of the most difficult examinations I had ever taken and by the time I was through writing it, I was 100% certain that I had NOT come anywhere close to the necessary requirements for acceptance into the University of Toronto. But, to my utter amazement, I was not only accepted, but I also did well academically and I finished the program in the shortest time possible. At that time, the part-time degree required 21 courses to be completed, which most people finished in four or five years. A number of people, myself included, decided to fast-track it and take two courses per semester for three semesters per year. This meant that we finished in 3½ years.

I thought I had worked hard to get an electrical engineering degree, but working full-time and taking a graduate degree at night brought it to a new level. I have never worked so hard in my life, and was forced to become an exceptional time manager. Often, many good disciplines like time management are created by necessity in difficult times, rather than being built through willpower when there is no pressure. It's competition that brings out the best in us. I was literally managing every minute of time of my life. Zero distractions, no downtime, no hobbies, no family time; just a fanatical dedication to getting it done.

I even suggested to my wife that she go back to school as well, since she would not see much of me for the next three years anyways. She did and she successfully completed a Master of Science degree, also from the University of Toronto, before we started a family. This joint decision made time management easier for both of us since our goals were aligned, and it reduced friction that would have naturally arisen.

I stuck with my schedule, knowing I was making an investment today that would pay off in the future. I stuck with routine and said no to most activities that weren't absolutely critical to the achievement of my goal. While I did not appreciate it at the time, I was being forced to learn the habits of being productive and time efficient. The MBA program had shifted and transformed my consciousness by pushing me well beyond my perceived and self-imposed limits. Without a doubt, this shift in my thinking was the most profound impact of the program, and it generated the potential for even greater accomplishments in the future.

The benefit from the big trials in life is rarely the expected outcome; rather, it's how we grow as a person and how we raise our performance in unexpected ways. Over 110 students had started the program at the same time as me, and only a handful of us finished it in the minimum 3½-year fast-track period. It was the most time-intensive period of my life.

At that time, it was less than 10 years since my epiphany and embarked upon the achievement of my five big goals. I had an electrical engineering degree and an MBA, I was happily married with a child on the way, and I was building my career with a great company.

As I incrementally improved each day and aggressively pursued my goals, my vision was turning into reality. I was only starting to realize the power of compounding effort; however, my confidence was rising and I was starting to see a pattern emerge. *Set a big goal, put your head down and do your best each day to achieve it, and then one day (eventually) you put your head up and you have accomplished something important.*

These small, daily and incremental improvements worked, and I began to achieve big and important goals.

HABIT 33

MAKE YOUR MORNING ROUTINE POWERFUL

"Each morning is a fresh beginning. We are, as it were, just beginning life. We have it entirely in our own hands. And when the morning with its fresh beginning comes, all yesterdays should be yesterdays, with which we have nothing to do. Sufficient is it to know that the way we lived our yesterday has determined for us our today. And, again, when the morning with its fresh beginning comes, all tomorrows should be tomorrows, with which we have nothing to do. Sufficient to know that the way we live our today determines our tomorrow." | Ralph Waldo Trine

Mornings are powerful. We are physically fresh, clear mentally, and ready to start a new day. This time sets the tone for the entire day. I like to get up early, between 5 am and 6 am, seven days a week. I started this habit in university when I needed to squeeze in some extra time to successfully finish my degree. Later, it became necessary for the various executive roles I held as I built my career, and now it's a habit.

No matter how difficult the previous day, a new morning tends to take the edge off and give you a better perspective.

Over the years, I have tried several different techniques to consistently get up early while getting optimal sleep. *The best technique I have found is to get up at the same time every morning, no matter what time I go to bed.*

This method enables the body to self-regulate. If you only get a few hours of sleep one night, due to an early rise one morning, you are naturally more tired and tend to go to bed earlier the next night, to meet the same early rise the next morning. I do this by setting my alarm to 6 am every day. I am almost always up well in advance of the alarm and turn it off. Sometimes I go weeks without the alarm ever sounding.

Resolve to get up at the same time each day, seven days a week, by setting your alarm to a specific time. Move it beyond your reach if necessary, and when it goes off, get up. Don't think about it too much; get up and get started. At night, reverse the process and try to go to bed near the same time each night, seven days a week.

Once I am up, I find it best to use the first hour or so to focus on a single project for my own personal improvement. I avoid using this time for email or other administrative tasks since they tend to clutter the mind. Instead, I use this time to elevate my thinking or my body. I will usually read something that inspires me or improves my mind, or I use the time for exercise. This helps me set the tone for the day, brings me to a higher state of attentiveness and improves my creativity.

After some quiet time and perhaps exercise, I believe it is critical to set a written schedule for the day. This is my transition to the working day. I have used this extra hour to invigorate my mind or my body, which will propel me through the ups and downs of the day. By transitioning to a schedule, I am setting myself up for success, with more energy and focus, but with a specific plan of what needs to be done. With this early rise and the careful use of my first hour, I transition into an exceptional day.

HABIT 34

STICK TO A WRITTEN SCHEDULE

"Either you run the day, or the day runs you." | Jim Rohn

Time is a precious resource that needs to be treated with great respect. Leverage time by establishing, and sticking to, *a written schedule* for the entire day: a schedule focused on achieving your highest priorities. These priorities should support your annual action plans, which are the means to attain your future goals.

A great schedule should include the following:

Focus on Outcomes, Not Activities. Your schedule should be focused on achieving specific outcomes that move you forward, not only activities that give the impression of momentum. Each scheduled item should be described as an outcome, and have sufficient time allocated to achieve it. For instance, rather than writing 'Meet with accountant,' use 'Decision on tax strategy.'

Avoid Distractions. Avoid any activity or person that is unproductive and consumes your valuable time. This is another critical reason to create your own schedule, since nature abhors a vacuum. If you do not fill your schedule with something important to <u>you</u>, other people will fill it with something important to <u>them</u>.

Allocate All Your Time. Plan your entire day, from when you get up in the morning until you go to sleep at night. Most of us tend to be very tightly scheduled during the workday but loosen the schedule during our own time. Avoid this. Mornings, evenings and weekends are incredibly important for our personal, financial, social and family development. Be specific with your non-work time, even if it is to schedule family time, reading or a workout; you will be more inclined to actually do it and avoid time-wasters like TV or excessive screen time.

Schedule Important or Difficult Tasks First. Schedule the very difficult, unpleasant or tough tasks earlier in the day. We tend to be fresh in the morning and have greater fortitude to get hard things done.

Pick a Single Major Accomplishment for the Day. By focusing on at least one major item that must be completed that day we naturally turn our backs on minor distractions and disruptions. Significant tasks invariably take more time than expected, as minor complications arise along the way. Focus on one major accomplishment each day and you'll find that you achieve more.

Establish a Routine that Works for You. Establish a regular morning routine, which may include a workout, meditation or a special project. Routines establish good habits, which are the foundation for achievement.

Schedule Some Form of Daily Exercise. Even if it is only walking the dog, do it, as muscle atrophy sets in very quickly. So, leaving room for regular daily exercise in your schedule is a must, even if it's just 15 minutes.

Make Your Schedule Easy to Use. Keep it simple, regularly accessible and easy to modify. Follow it closely throughout the day and it will make you more productive and satisfied with the accomplishment of your work.

HABIT 35

AVOID TIME-CONSUMING PEOPLE AND ACTIVITIES

"The person who says it cannot be done should not interrupt the person who is doing it." | Chinese proverb

Time is a limited and precious commodity. It is much more valuable than money, since you can always create more money but you cannot create more time.

We each are given a fixed amount of time to improve our family, business, health and welfare. While we know when our life started, we don't know when it will end. Therefore, it is absolutely critical to achieve the important things in life and not waste a minute, by getting into the habit of using our time wisely. I am not simply referring to a schedule, but to a mindset where you avoid any time-consuming people and activities.

Eliminating time wasters starts with clarifying the difference between being busy and being productive. It's more than getting rid of excessive relaxation, media consumption or leisure activities. Instead, it's about focusing on those activities that give you the greatest results for the least amount of effort.

To develop this habit, do the following:

Be Selective. Get used to rejecting most activities that are not directly aligned with your major goals. Say no to <u>most</u> requests from people, particularly if they involve any expenditure of time, resources or money.

Be Tough. Develop a thick skin. In the short run you will not be making many new friends, but you will be gaining respect and increasing your time bank.

Be Discerning. If you do agree to requests, make sure your time commitment can be significantly reduced. For example, if someone requests a testimonial or letter of reference from you, tell him or her to craft the first draft and send it to you for revision.

Be Fair. Use your judgment in each case and always treat people with respect and dignity. Don't deny requests that are necessary or that are significant to the welfare of others, even if it is an inconvenience for you.

Be Focused. Focus on the few critical things that produce exponential results, and outsource everything else, so you can avoid all the minutiae and trivia that tends to consume a day. Use these critical few items to generate wealth, enabling you to outsource even more in the future.

Be Sincere. Before beginning an activity, ask yourself "If this were my last day, would I do what I am about to do?" If you keep asking yourself this question, it will drive you toward activities and people that create opportunity, instead of those that needlessly consume your time and resources.

Be Honorable. If you do accept a request, be honorable and fulfill your commitments to the maximum of your ability.

HABIT 36

DO THE MOST IMPORTANT THINGS FIRST

"The best time to plant a tree was 20 years ago. The second best time is now." | Chinese proverb

Procrastination is the thief of time and dreams, and it is one of the worst habits we develop as human beings. The amount of human potential, energy and accomplishment lost to procrastination is truly astounding. We all do it to one degree or another, and we have all suffered its consequences. It is often a habit that develops in childhood and becomes worse later in life if it isn't nipped in the bud.

Overcoming procrastination is truly a lifelong chore for most people, myself included. We tell ourselves that we procrastinate for very good reasons: too much work, the need to focus on more important priorities, the lack of necessary resources, etc. The reality is that this insidious habit is driven largely by fear, upbringing, laziness, emotion and lack of self-discipline.

We know, both intuitively and practically, that the only way we can truly achieve our big goals and succeed is by doing difficult things that are necessary but unpleasant. For instance, in sales, it may be cold calling; in parenting, it may be disciplining; in health, it may be exercising; in nutrition, it may be eating fruits and vegetables. All of these may be unpleasant, but necessary.

One of the best ways to do these difficult and important things is to do them when we are fresh and most productive. For most people, this tends to be the morning. We all have different circadian rhythms (our natural sleep-wake cycle) and different times when we work best. Often, difficult activities take longer than expected, so you might as well get started first thing in the morning.

Don't overanalyze when you need to do something hard. While it is necessary to think through the first step, start right away with what you have in front of you at that moment. The circumstances will never be perfect. After a few minutes of action, you will get traction as your mind becomes attuned to the idea of forward momentum. You have used your willpower to override your internal resistance to the task and your momentum will continue to build. Stay focused on the task until it is completed—not 80% or 90%, but 100% complete.

Another simple way to overcome the habit of procrastination is to build momentum by doing one thing each day that you have been putting off. Big or small, each day, commit to doing at least one thing that you have been putting off, and then do it. Make it a priority to get it done. Do not overthink it; look beyond any fears and get it done quickly and completely.

HABIT 37

CREATE A PRODUCTIVE ENVIRONMENT

"We become what we think about all day." | Ralph Waldo Emerson

Our environment has a large effect on the development of good habits. Where we live, work and travel during a 24-hour period has a significant impact on our actions and progress. For instance, visiting a new environment for even a short period of time elicits a broad range of strong emotions that can have a profound and often life-changing impact.

There are many examples of people or entire societies that have undergone profound changes as a result of their changing environment. It can be as simple as a student moving away to university for the first time, or a society being transformed as the result of war, a natural calamity or economic transition.

If you are not happy with your environment, change it immediately. Do not wait a minute to make it better. Find ways to make it more productive, cleaner, better and reflective of the type of person you want to become, instead of the person you are today.

For Home: Make your home a place of peace and tranquility, where you can rest, be refreshed and spend quality time with those you love.

Find ways to keep it well organized, so it helps you achieve both your personal and professional goals. Make room in your budget for outside help and get rid of anything extraneous. Purge all artifacts that hinder progress, and keep your environment simple. Live as close to possible to your work, since commuting is a zero-value-added activity that robs you of your valuable time. Create a special space at home that is yours and yours alone. Meditate and relax there, since that is where many of your best ideas will come.

For Work: Keep your work environment in a style that fits you and reflects your goals and habits of the future, not today. Seek simplicity, while making it productive for you, and your style, not others. Minimize the potential for disruption, loss of productivity or distractions. Personalize your space with inspirational quotes, your goals and good books. This is where many of your goals will be achieved, so make it a place of maximum productivity. It is meant for work, not relaxation, and it should reflect that fact.

For Travel: Travel as often as your budget allows. It is one of the best ways to get a new and vastly improved perspective, particularly if you travel to a place of exceptional beauty or inspiration. Avoid going to the same place every year because it's a habit. Seek new places, new adventures and new people, particularly those in alignment with the achievement of your goals. Soak in the culture and learn as much as you can to bring back home and help you become better.

Take your environment very seriously! Do not fall into a rut and assume that it is good enough. Every one of your senses is stimulated during your waking hours, and this reinforces certain beliefs, good or bad. Your environment will reflect your self-image. *A positive, progressive and organized environment is usually the sign of a positive, progressive and organized person.*

HABIT 38

LEARN TO SAY NO FREQUENTLY

*"No one ever went broke by saying
no too often."* | Harvey Mackay

Developing good habits is largely an exercise in overcoming and redirecting human nature. Human nature is the internal guidance system driven by evolutionary and genetic forces designed to ensure we survive as a species. Good habits guide and control these forces. Human nature is like the engine in a moving car, always turning over while habits are like the controls (steering wheels, brakes, accelerator, etc.). Using your controls to make constant minor adjustments allows you to direct the car to a specific and productive goal.

While driving, you are engaged in three tasks simultaneously. First, you are focused on where you are going, by watching the road immediately in front of you, knowing that it leads to a specific location ahead. Second, you are constantly correcting your course to keep moving in your intended direction. Third, you are avoiding obstacles and distractions in order to avoid being stopped or slowed down in any way. *This combination of being focused on your target, saying yes to what you can control, and no to what you cannot control is also the essence of developing good habits.*

Saying no is often the most difficult of the three actions, since it regularly involves not doing something enjoyable, or annoying and disappointing people—often those we know and care for. Saying no is hard, since it moves us away from pleasure (e.g., food, relaxation or digital distractions) and toward things that are difficult but important (e.g., work, exercise or helping others). Developing the habit of saying no to people is often tricky since it is in our human nature to socially connect with people for resources and protection. However, if you develop the habit of saying no more frequently, you regain control of your circumstances and eliminate the risk of running off the road completely.

Prevent the Request. Make saying no the rule, not the exception. You need to set the expectations of people around you about your own boundary conditions, so they understand what they can and cannot request of you. This is primarily focused on your immediate and extended family, friends and workmates. It's best to be direct but diplomatic, so you prevent the request in the first place. For instance, my family knows not to call me during the workday about a personal matter (unless it's an emergency). Perhaps you have certain hours of the workday dedicated to sales calls or prospecting, and your colleagues know not to interrupt you during that time.

Reframe the Request. Another easy way to say no is to remind yourself that most requests are for your resources, usually time or money or attention. Therefore, if you can reframe the situation so that by saying no you are actually preserving resources that can be used for the most important things in your life, it becomes easier to say. For instance, saying no to a request to meet someone for coffee is really saying yes to an extra hour to work on a project to help your business, family or job. You are not being selfish, only smart and dedicated to productive activities. Of course, there are often times when saying yes to a meeting is critically important; use your discretion and good judgment.

Deny the Request. Courage lies at the root of good actions, while fear drives away confidence, causing us to shrink in the face of opportunity. If you get a request and know it will not work, buck up the courage to say no as soon as you hear it or read it. Don't be rude, but get the words out fast so you can get the situation behind you as quickly as possible. If the situation requires more consideration and you still decide no, respond promptly and diplomatically. Avoid giving an explanation if possible; say it does not work and move on. A quick yes or no is usually respected and appreciated by busy, productive people.

Saying no is not about being difficult, rude or uncooperative, even if others perceive it that way. It is about your priorities. Saying no when necessary enables you to say yes to the things that are the most meaningful and most important to you.

ACTIONS FOR TRACTION

What morning routine invigorates your mind and helps you prepare for the day?

_____

_____

_____

Be honest: do you make a written schedule every day? If not, how would you start one now?

_____

_____

_____

What is one thing you need to say no to each day, in order to be more productive?

_____

_____

_____

How can you prevent unreasonable requests for your precious resources?

_____

_____

_____

CHAPTER 7

MAKING EFFECTIVE DECISIONS

"Once you make a decision, the universe conspires to make it happen." | Ralph Waldo Emerson

MY STORY: CAREER FORK IN THE ROAD

As careers progress, decisions become more complex and difficult, stakes get higher, and the time to correct mistakes shortens. Effective decision-making, or good judgment, becomes more crucial with the passing of time, as the impact of our decisions influence more people and decision-making prowess tends to solidify.

While the cumulative impact of small, minor, daily decisions is important, it is the big, sporadic decisions that require exceptional judgment. These are the decisions that need more thought, objective review and critical analysis. The cumulative impact of these big decisions can be profound over your lifetime, particularly relating to health, wealth and relationships.

I had been at Ford for five years when I finished my MBA, and my career was going very well. My wife had just finished her Master of

Science Degree at the University of Toronto, and I had been offered a new role with Ford. With our formal education complete and our first child on the way, I was at a career fork in the road. It was time for a decision.

My long-term plan had always included moving back to Vancouver so I could be closer to my extended family and build my career there, and I was now thinking this would be a good time to do it. I thought long and hard about this decision, as I wanted it to be based on fact, not emotion. I asked myself what was the worst that could happen if I moved to Vancouver, and I looked at the pros and cons of that decision. The biggest risk was economic, as Vancouver did not have the same career opportunities as Toronto. However, as I already had five years of experience and recently completed my MBA, I viewed this as a good time to make a change and was prepared for a transition.

Ultimately, if the right choice is clear, the decision is easy (a non-decision, really). However, when the right choice is unclear, then experience, expertise and intuition play important roles in sound judgment.

There were a number of factors in play for the year leading up to our decision, such as schooling for our first child, the price of real estate (Toronto was experiencing a real estate price boom at the time), career opportunities and lifestyle for our family.

I did not know it at the time, but these factors had been percolating in my mind for many months, helping prepare me for a better decision. With complex decisions, rarely is there one overriding factor that influences the final outcome. It is usually the minor factors and the interrelationship between them that is significant. We reviewed those factors closely. We ultimately trusted our intuition that things would work out well, and decided it was best to move.

To commit to our decision, my wife and I decided to first buy a house in Vancouver, rent it out and then move in later. I flew out and had five days to buy a house. I looked at a number of properties, made offers on two or three, and ultimately settled on a nice bungalow in North Vancouver. I immediately turned around, rented out the property, and flew back to Toronto. We had now laid the groundwork to return home to Vancouver.

The next thing I needed to do was to quit my job at Ford and get a job in Vancouver. By having the intention of making the move, the rest fell into place. I had given myself a deadline as to when I was going to move, and even though I didn't have a new job yet, I went to see my boss at Ford and told him my intention to quit and move to Vancouver. He was disappointed, but as soon as he heard Vancouver he said, "Vancouver? You must be kidding! There was someone in here this morning looking for a manager to help run a plant out in Vancouver. Why don't you give him a call?" He handed me the business card of a corporate recruiter, and I went back to my office to call the recruiter. I went through a long series of interviews and ultimately accepted the job offer. *Now, I know this good luck does not happen often, but opportunity certainly does favor the prepared mind. Events can conspire to support our intentions, particularly if the decision has been fully embraced in our mind and heart. The rest is detail.*

After giving the tenants notice to vacate, we moved permanently from Toronto into our new home in North Vancouver and started our family. And while there were definitely difficulties and significant obstacles, once we had decided on this course of action, we did not second-guess ourselves. We did not judge ourselves, but made the best of our circumstances. Through thick and thin, through good and bad, I was determined to make the decision work and provide a comfortable, safe, prosperous and secure environment for me and my family, which continues to this day.

HABIT 39

ADOPT A DECISION-MAKING SYSTEM

"The most difficult thing is the decision to act,
the rest is merely tenacity." | Amelia Earhart

Decision-making is, and will continue to be, a critical part of your personal and professional development. Throughout your career, you will be faced with many decisions, both large and small, that will have a significant and material impact on your life.

These decisions will affect your financial, health and family situation in a profound way and will either help you achieve your long-term goals or hold you back. I am referring to significant decisions, not routine or mundane ones. Significant decisions are often affected by external pressures and deadlines, while mundane decisions are made on our own time. For instance, a marriage proposal or business proposition will have a relatively short shelf life since there are others involved who have a vested interest in a timely decision.

By having a decision-making system, you can make the decision relatively quickly, without undue influence and with a more rational or objective approach. Since decisions should be made quickly and changed slowly, a simple and effective tool will get it done, enabling you to move on with action.

The best approach I have come across and continue to use personally is attributed to Benjamin Franklin. His decision-making system was to make a list of the decision pros and cons on a piece of paper, and add to it over the course of three or four days as additional ideas came to his mind. Then he would cross out pros and cons that seemed equal to each other in importance; for instance, if one pro was equivalent to three cons, he would strike out all four points. If, after another day or two, no new ideas came to him, he would review the remaining items on the list, weigh the difference between the remaining pros and cons, and then decide accordingly.

The beauty of this system is its simple and rational approach. By writing down the pros and cons for several days, you have sufficient time to consider multiple factors, and you maintain a written account of your thinking over time, not at one point in time. It also enables the rational weighing of pros and cons, without the emotional lenses we often bring to our decisions.

No system is flawless; however, the key is to have a system. For example, asking your friend or neighbor for help is not a system. It may result in an uninformed and uncommitted opinion, and it's you who will have to live with the result. I am not suggesting that you create a decision-making matrix for every decision, only for those times when the stakes are high and you truly want to consider all the relevant facts before making a final decision.

Do not discount the role of intuition in your decision-making, or the input of trusted advisers, mentors, or members of your *Mastermind* (See Habit 67 for more information about a *Mastermind*). These factors can be invaluable in helping you become a better decision-maker, by leveraging your collective experiences of successes and failures.

Be mindful that not making a decision at that moment is in itself a decision—a decision to maintain the status quo. The status quo option often has great appeal, since it's familiar and comfortable, and, in many cases, it is the best approach. However, make that decision knowingly and with full consideration of its implications. Otherwise, use this decision-making framework to make better decisions, achieve greater progress and gain results.

HABIT 40

DECIDE BASED ON FACT, NOT EMOTION

"When you cannot make up your mind which of two evenly balanced courses of action you should take—choose the bolder." | William Joseph Slim

Life is a series of decision-making events, interspersed with living with the implications of those decisions. We make dozens of minor decisions throughout the day. Most are trivial; however, we are periodically faced with more significant decisions. At these critical points, emotions like fear, jealousy and enthusiasm can enter the scene and cloud our ability to make effective decisions. The problem is compounded by suggestions from well-meaning (though sometimes uninformed) friends, family members and colleagues. In the end, we often make decisions based on emotions, but justify them with logic.

I believe there is a better way. Seek out as many of the hard facts as possible in the time available to you, and use them to help make the decision. Facts have a way of irritating us with their objectivity, and they are hard to obtain, can be difficult to understand and are often at odds with our own preference. However, they speak the truth and ultimately guide us in making better decisions.

You will discover that those facts are surprisingly hard to find for several reasons. First, since so few people actually take a fact-based approach to solving problems, there is not a lot of demand for factual information. Second, most people and organizations prefer sharing opinions, not facts. As their objective may be to confuse or influence you as part of a sales process, they may be motivated to hide or distort the facts. Third, in our Information Age, it is much easier to disseminate opinion than fact. Finally, it's simply plain hard work.

Good sources of facts are:

- Unbiased, third-party, independent organizations such as research bureaus, professional standards bodies and certain regulatory organizations.

- Unbiased, third-party, independent professionals such as auditors, researchers and independent analysts.

- Your own independent, source-based research, based on interviews with people close to the situation or on the examination of source materials.

Be wary when facts are presented to you, particularly if you are being sold in a transaction. If there is any doubt in your mind (and there should be), ask for the source of the information and check it yourself. It is good practice to periodically source-check facts anyway, as you will be astonished by how often they are wrong, misleading or distorted.

Avoid the temptation to jump to hasty conclusions based on partial, unsubstantiated information, no matter how much pressure you are under to make a decision. The decision can usually wait until you have sufficient information to make an informed decision, and if it can't, then it may be best to pass on it altogether.

The process of seeking the facts often introduces us to people who are much more knowledgeable about a given situation and can add considerably to the decision-making process. While seeking facts may slightly delay the actual decision, this time is usually well spent if the resulting decision is sound and prevents you from wasting time on fixing the results of a poor decision later. Better to do it right the first time and avoid costly and time-consuming mistakes.

HABIT 41

VERIFY AND THEN TRUST

*"Love all, trust a few, do wrong
to none."* | *William Shakespeare*

We all know that trust is the basis of any good relationship and that high levels of trust can make a relationship incredibly strong over time. Trust has a way of removing obstacles and shortening time, by allowing others to become more responsible for the things that are important to us. We trust our children, health, finances and lives in the hands of teachers, doctors, accountants, friends and family on a daily basis.

Normally, we grant this trust to others slowly based on a number of different factors: our own previous experiences with them in less important matters; recommendations from other individuals whom we already trust; proxies for trust such as organizations, brands or institutions; and finally, with our personal discretion. These approaches are sound, rational and work <u>most</u> of the time.

The problem arises, however, when we lead with our hearts, not our heads: when we form the habit of automatically granting trust, rather than letting it be earned. We do this because it is the easy, inoffensive, likable and expedient way of building relationships with others. We want to accelerate the relationship building process, often so we can be liked or gain some advantage, and thus we may move too quickly into granting trust. We skip right over skepticism, ignoring red flags, and can be encouraged by others who have their own trust-building agendas aimed squarely at us.

We can bypass any form of verification since we become overly concerned about what others may think of us, particularly those people who may hold positions of authority or influence, and who could make us look like fools for even doubting their integrity. For example, how many times have you signed a simple contract without actually reading the entire document because you were told it was boilerplate or 'our standard agreement'? Or, how often have you received an estimate for contract work (on your house, car, etc.), only to find the actual cost to be substantially different than the estimate and, miraculously, almost always higher? Or you trust someone with some work or task, only to find out later that there were additional hidden fees or other undisclosed costs and complications?

Developing a healthy level of skepticism is a good way to raise your awareness that a risk needs to be mitigated, particularly in high-stakes situations involving your health, reputation, family, business or finances. The higher the potential risk, the more aware you must become, and hence the greater the need for verification.

Like any good habit, it takes constant awareness, diligence and practice to verify information. More importantly, it takes skill to assess when and how much effort to put into verifying information, a person or an action.

Here are some guidelines that will be helpful to you:

Be a Healthy Skeptic. Operate with the mindset that the initial information you receive may be faulty at best, if not a distortion or a downright fabrication, particularly if you are on the receiving end of a request for money, time or some other form of precious resource. Assume that much of what you read, or even see, may be unreliable or distorted, and not an absolute representation of the truth.

Be Wary of Secondhand Information. Be wary of information being passed on to you, since many people do not do their own fact-checking or independent verification, and so inadvertently pass on false or misleading information with the conviction that it is correct. Their level of belief in the soundness of this information may influence you to believe it as well, even though they themselves do not actually know it is wrong and the underlying premise is incorrect.

Actually Read It First. Get into the practice of reading each document you sign in its entirety, and never be rushed into signing something you do not read. If you are not allowed sufficient time to read it, even if it takes overnight, walk away. This includes standard documents, such as warranty returns, brief contracts and so-called 'boilerplate' terms and conditions. *If you sign it, read it!*

Verify Claims. When possible, particularly when the stakes are high, go to primary sources of information to verify claims. Ask for supporting documentation and independent, third-party verification, or directly verify the primary sources yourself.

Learn How Audits Work. In business, understand how financial, safety and quality auditing works, and then put procedures in place to ensure they are effective. Systems like ISO (International Organization for Standards) are great ways of verifying your own business systems.

Change Routines. Periodically change a habit or routine, particularly if you suspect deception. Many accounting frauds have been exposed when a temporary accountant fills in, or a new auditor is appointed.

Go to the Source. Get as close to the primary sources of data as possible, even if you have to do some unconventional things to get the information, such as talking directly to the person doing the job, calling suppliers of primary materials or services, visiting addresses shown on documents, or asking for original copies of documents.

I believe that most people are good, honest and hardworking. However, even good, honest and hardworking people can have poor information and unknowingly pass it on to you. In addition, there are a few unsavory people in the world, so you owe it to yourself and your family to take the steps necessary for proper protection, and to ensure you do not become a victim simply because you became too trusting. *The closer you are to the truth, the better off you will be and the more trust you can grant in the long run.*

HABIT 42

ASK YOURSELF WHAT IS THE WORST THAT COULD HAPPEN

"Every strike brings me closer to the next home run." | Babe Ruth

Many of our biggest regrets, and our most significant conquests, can be traced back to how we either succumbed to, or mastered, fear. Fear lies at the root of our inaction and learning how to master it is a critical skill in the real world of progress.

The problem is that fear becomes a mental monster of our own creation that is vastly out of proportion with the facts of the situation, and that can drive subsequent paralysis and worry. Prolonged paralysis reinforces our focus on the very source of the paralysis in the first place: **the fear**, rather than our desired outcome, **the intention**.

When gripped by fear and worry, it is important to understand your emotions so they can be dealt with more objectively and calmly.

One of the best ways to accomplish this is to ask yourself "What is the absolute worst thing that can happen in this situation?" By asking this question, you will find that the worst that can happen is often not that bad. And that's the worst that can happen—not the best, or even the most likely!

This whole mental process is a way of taming fear and bringing rational context to a problem. This analytical process tends to clarify your thinking; your creative intelligence tends to kick in, and a solution appears.

Say, for example, that you are eager for a job promotion and plan to discuss it with your boss, but you are fearful. You believe the worst that can happen is that you will lose precious family time if you get the promotion. This may impact your effectiveness and get you fired.

A creative solution would be to ask your boss to work out a flexible schedule arrangement that decreases the impact on your family. Another creative step would be to ask your boss to clarify the commitment required prior to taking on the role, to see if it would truly have a significant impact on your family. Finally, you could talk to your spouse to see if there is something he or she can do to share the workload at home and decrease the impact on the family.

We have a tendency to make monsters out of our fear, making it look much worse than it really is. By asking yourself "What is the worst that can happen?", the fear monster gets tamed, and we can make decisions in a more calm, productive and rational state, leading to better results and more success.

HABIT 43

ASK THE PERSON MOST LIKELY TO HAVE THE ANSWER

"The only real failure in life is not to be true to the best one knows." | *Buddha*

We are living in a self-help culture, and there are plenty of people who are more than happy to give us unsolicited advice. Often, this advice is worth what you paid for it: *zero.*

Don't automatically seek assistance from people you feel most comfortable talking to or enjoy spending time with; instead, find the person most likely to have the answer you need!

So how do you go about finding those who are likely to have the right answer?

Make a Clear and Precise Request. Determine exactly what question you need to have answered. Be sure that you don't already have the answer and just don't like it, so you are looking for 'a different, right answer' that is more to your liking. Be sure that the answer you are looking for is important to your life, and that it's worth spending the time and effort to find it.

Find the Very Best People in the Field. My rule of thumb in finding these people is to look for someone 10X more successful than me in a particular area. This can be a high standard and it refocuses my attention on a few people who are often outside of my personal or professional network. For example, if I am looking for some financial advice on a certain investment approach, I need to find someone who is 10X more successful than me or who has grown that particular financial asset 10X more than I have. It is not good enough to just find someone with experience; find the critical few people who are the experts in that field.

Listen Carefully to the Advice and Only Act if It Works for You. Thank the person who gave the advice because chances are that you will need that person again. Offer to help them in some way.

I strongly recommend that you avoid seeking advice from the people you are most comfortable talking to, unless they truly do have a solid understanding of the subject and proven experience in getting results. This is particularly difficult to do with your friends and family, as they will want to offer advice and be part of making the decision. They have good intentions, but their information may not serve you well.

HABIT 44

TRUST YOUR INTUITION

*"I am not a product of my circumstances.
I am a product of my decisions."* | Stephen Covey

Decision-making is rarely a rational exercise, as we don't always have the complete set of information necessary to decide well. It is usually an irrational process, with an overlay of rationality to give us emotional comfort. As you accumulate experience over time, you will learn to depend less on the objective side of decision-making and more on the intuitive side, until it becomes a habit.

In a decision-making information vacuum, the difficulty is to discern between emotion and intuition. I believe intuition is drawn from previous similar experiences that enable us to recall lessons or extrapolate results in a way that gives us additional guidance. Emotional decisions are based on our human nature and on undisciplined forces that trigger negative behaviors.

Trusting intuition does not come easily, since are often overwhelmed by human nature (e.g., fight or flight response) or we become frozen with fear. In addition, we will use confirmation bias (the tendency to seek or see only information to support a view) to seek out more information to justify the decisions we have already made in our heads, rather than going with the sparse data and feelings in our hearts. We need evidence that our intuition works. With time, we determine after the fact whether or not it worked. We use that feedback to improve our intuition once again.

If you have not developed a high level of intuitive decision-making yet, don't be hard on yourself. Be mindful of it over time and develop confidence in your inner strong voice as you trust it to help you make decisions. How do you go about doing that, practically?

Try the following:

Start Small. Get into the habit of making rapid decisions on small matters, so you start to trust yourself more. Don't overthink any small decision. Respond rapidly, particularly if you have a strong intuitive feeling about it.

Be Positive. Fear heightens our insecurities or negativity, forcing us to seek more certainty when it may not exist. Stay positive and intuition will rise up within you more naturally.

Be Self-Aware. Be more aware of your emotional state or mindset when making important decisions, and then determine how much of the feeling is rooted in fear or courage. *Never make a significant decision when you are in a highly emotional state.*

Don't Overanalyze. Go with the best information you have in the time available, and then move forward.

If you go with intuition and it doesn't work out, try to figure out what let you down. Take the time to make improvements. Like any habit, it takes continuous practice over a long period of time to make it stick. Intuition is one of those soft skills that can be critical in decision-making, and understanding it can really help you avoid making material and costly mistakes.

HABIT 45

DECIDE SWIFTLY AND CHANGE YOUR MIND SLOWLY

"Changing our decision sets up a bad habit. It reinforces decision-making as an expression of bewilderment and ignorance, instead of wisdom and freedom." | Sakyong Mipham

Decision-making is at the heart of everything we do personally, professionally, mentally and physically. Even for external events outside our control, we still need to decide how to respond. Decisions are everywhere and will be for the rest of your life!

There are three critical parts to every decision:

1. Decision-making (process).

2. Decision quality (outcome).

3. Decision longevity (perseverance).

Most people focus on the first two critical parts of the decision—the process and the outcome—but overlook the habit of sticking with a decision once it is made. Making a good decision is only half the work because there is always a risk that it can be undone over time by you, by others or by circumstances. If you stick to your decision halfheartedly, you will be worse off than if you had made no decision at all, since you will be deluded into a sense of progress when none exists.

Once a Decision Is Made, Implement It Immediately. Don't hesitate, not even a moment. Take some immediate action that will start to build momentum from that point forward. Try to take actions that will declare your commitment to the decision publicly, either with your family, friends or business associates. This will make you even more committed to its fulfillment.

Commit by Taking Early Actions that Will Make Retreat Impossible. Forward momentum will become irreversible, making it very difficult, if not impossible, to go backward.

Start Investing Resources into the Successful Implementation of the Decision. The greater the resource commitment to a process, the greater the likelihood of a successful outcome.

Make Your Decision Meaningful. Focus on a higher purpose and the reasons behind the decision, so it gives you energy and a zest for its successful conclusion. No one can get excited about trivial and unimportant things.

Don't Abandon a Decision When the Going Gets Tough. When the urge to abandon your decision starts to well up inside you, pause momentarily, tell your inner voice "Thank You" and move on. Don't feed the beast by focusing on your fears. Stay focused on your intention.

ACTIONS FOR TRACTION

Describe your system for making major decisions.

_____

_____

_____

What is your biggest fear when making a major decision? What are three things you can do to reduce that fear?

_____

_____

_____

Describe a good decision you have made lately, and how you made it.

_____

_____

_____

What is a big question you are facing right now? Who is the one person who is most likely to have the answer?

_____

_____

_____

CHAPTER 8

LEARNING TO LEAD

"A leader is one who knows the way, goes the way and shows the way." | John C. Maxwell

MY STORY: TRIAL BY FIRE

My first real business leadership role came when I was recruited, joined and ultimately ran a fiber optic cable company. I had managed people before and had titles that indicated I was in a leadership position; however, I had never really *learned to lead*.

I was hired as a Production Superintendent at Pirelli Cables (Surrey plant), a high-volume copper and fiber optic telecommunications cable manufacturing facility, located in Surrey, British Columbia, Canada. It was a subsidiary of Pirelli SpA, the global Italian industrial juggernaut, better known for its tires and calendars than for cable making.

The plant had been built in the 1970s and, while the workforce was highly skilled and motivated, by the early 1990s the business had lost its ability to compete globally. In addition, a new plant had just been built by Pirelli in South Carolina, putting more pressure on the Surrey plant to perform better.

We were responsible for manufacturing fiber optic and copper telecommunications cable for Canada and some international markets. The plant was a large facility (about 150,000 square feet), with about 140 employees (approximately 30 in the office and 110 in the plant). It was a very fast-paced environment with sales in the $60 million to $90 million range per year.

After about one year as a Production Superintendent, I was promoted to Plant Manager, and given full profit and loss responsibility for the business. Given my previous experience at Ford Electronics, which had also been a very fast-paced, innovative manufacturing business, the Pirelli management felt I had what it took to return the plant to a solid financial footing. The strategic goals were to transition the business from producing both copper and fiber optic cable to solely producing fiber optic cable, and to achieve profitable growth. While the management was confident in me, I was less sure. *I had learned my first lesson in leadership: master fear and be courageous.*

I had been in the role of Plant Manager for a short number of days when I chaired my first management team meeting. I have a distinct memory of this first meeting, as I was sitting at the head of the table while the entire management team discussed various operational and financial issues. I became deeply engrossed in the conversation around a particularly difficult issue when suddenly somebody said, "OK, what's the decision?" At that point, all the heads turned to my end of the table. I looked up and saw everyone staring at me and thought to myself "Why are they looking at me?" before I realized that they were turning to me for their decision. *My second real lesson in leadership had arrived: leadership is about making the hard decisions, not the easy ones.*

I now knew this was going to be much more difficult than I had imagined, so I focused on the strategic goals of the company. My time at Ford had taught me a lot about low-cost, high-quality manufacturing. I also had learned about the power of innovation, particularly leveraging strategies to lower costs, raise margins, engage people and improve output. Finally, I knew my own limitations and started to depend heavily on my management team for support. *My third real lesson on leadership was being aware of my weaknesses and then building a great management team to overcome those weaknesses.*

While the people in both the office and manufacturing plant were great, it was a very challenging business environment. Demand was rising due to the infrastructure expansion of fiber optic cable for the internet backbone, prices were dropping dramatically, and we were a high-cost jurisdiction.

Ultimately, we restructured the business by selling off the copper cable product line and focusing solely on fiber optic cable manufacturing, where the process was more automated and demand was higher. We restructured every aspect of the business, including the operating structure, culture, technology and business systems, with a heavy emphasis on getting employees deeply involved in improving quality and production volumes while lowering costs.

It took some time, but with a small management team working together and the great support of the employees, we were able to turn the company around. We went from a significant monthly loss to a significant profit. We became one of the most productive and profitable Pirelli cable manufacturing facilities of the many around the world. While it took us close to five years to achieve those results, along the way I was on my own personal leadership journey of self-improvement.

The entire turnaround—the strong team, innovation, excellent systems and building a culture of excellence—really came down to a simple leadership lesson: *leading with courage while encouraging people to contribute to the best of their abilities.*

HABIT 46

ALWAYS ACT LIKE A LEADER

"Be a yardstick of quality. Some people aren't used to an environment where excellence is expected." | Steve Jobs

Whether we realize it or not, every one of us is a leader in some way: in our families, workplaces or communities. Whether your goal is to make money, create great art or contribute to your community, each of us benefits from developing leadership skills.

I believe great leaders have these four significant qualities:

They Are Great Communicators. Both internally (self-talk) and externally with those around them. They communicate in a way that inspires action and the achievement of big goals while encouraging others to excel.

They Are Dependable. Great leaders build trust over time by consistently delivering what they promise. They show the way forward by committing and then meeting that commitment, every time!

They Are Results-Oriented. The overarching goal of a leader is to achieve something important and meaningful, something that creates value and helps the world become a better place.

They Are Persons of Character. However they show it, leaders are first and foremost good people. If you trust their leadership, you should also be able to trust them without question.

To develop the habit of acting like a leader, do the following:

- Actively seek out any leadership positions where you can develop and practice your skills.

- Take some formal leadership training courses.

- Seek out a more experienced leader who can give you tips and suggestions on how to improve.

- Never refuse a challenging assignment. It builds leadership skills, and you might be surprised to find how much of a leader you already are.

- Seek the road less traveled, as it will provide resistance and build stronger leadership muscles.

- Focus on transferable people skills that can be moved from one sector, company and situation to another.

- Never quit!

HABIT 47

BUILD A WORLD-CLASS TEAM

*"Few things can help an individual more than to place
responsibility on him, and to let him know that you
trust him."* | Booker T. Washington

Great leaders know that significant accomplishments require exceptional teams. In business, we often talk about the importance of teams, but we don't always take the time necessary to truly plan an effective team.

How to Build a World-Class Team:

1. Focus on building the right team before the mission. By getting the right team in place first, people will feel that they are part of the bigger picture and be more committed to its achievement.

2. Build a superior branded company so that the best people come to you, rather than you going to find them. This saves time and money, and they tend to bring their top colleagues with them.

3. Build a team with the right people and skill sets that complement one another, and are necessary to achieve the task. Avoid hiring people who are like you or who share your

personality traits. Hire for the skills and traits necessary to achieve the mission.

4. Build a team that truly supports and trusts one another, so it's not a group of individuals, but rather a team with a common purpose. This process takes some time, because it requires the formation of the team, a period of time for them to get to know one another, for that knowing to turn into trust and, ultimately, for that trust to turn into action.

5. Ensure that each person on the team knows his or her role and responsibilities, and also that he or she will be held accountable for the execution of that role. Like a sports team, each person plays a particular role. They are supported by one another, but at the end of the day, each person has a position. As a leader, it is your responsibility to ensure that those roles and responsibilities are clearly defined, articulated, agreed to, measured and appropriately resourced over time.

6. A team needs to be rewarded for its actions. No one will work at a top level without some incentive, including being appreciated for a job well done, because most of us are focused on doing something important. So your reward should be consistent with the team's purpose.

HABIT 48

GET ANY COMMITMENT BY FOLLOWING THESE FOUR STEPS

"Until one is committed, there is hesitancy, the chance to draw back, always ineffectiveness." | William H. Murray

One of the questions I get asked frequently is "How do I get buy-in?"

In the business world, nobody goes immediately from a complete lack of awareness to 100% buy-in. It does not happen naturally, and it certainly doesn't happen just because a leader says so. In fact, many times I have seen cases where people are opposed to a good idea because a leader said it needed to be done, and they did not feel they had contributed to the solution.

I believe the best way to gain commitment from a person, or a group of people, in an organization is to move through a phased approach, as follows:

Phase 1: Unawareness to Awareness. Most people start with little or no awareness of a problem. While you as a leader are completely aware of your plans, goals and vision, most people are not. Get out of your bubble and talk to people. Your goal is to move them from unawareness to awareness, particularly if it is a significant problem that will require their support or cooperation. It still doesn't mean that they are ready to take any action, only that they are now aware.

Phase 2: Awareness to Understanding. Many of us are aware of issues but don't understand them fully, or we believe they only impact others, not ourselves. A leader needs to take the time to ensure people have the correct, clear information, and that they understand it and its implications. Provide opportunities for engagement, feedback and clarification.

Phase 3: Understanding to Commitment. That usually involves answering the question "What's in it for me?" If they see enough of what's in it for them, they will move to a state of greater commitment; if not, then the response tends to be neutral or negative.

Phase 4: Commitment to Action. At this point, most people are very receptive to doing something. Since they have gone through the previous three phases, they are aware there is a problem, they understand it fully and they see the implications for themselves. At this stage, they will be highly receptive to taking action. Ensure you articulate clearly what the action is, what their roles will be, how it's going to be achieved, how it's going to be measured, and what success looks like.

Most of us try to move our teams too quickly from a state of unawareness to action, bypassing the critical phases. Invariably, this leads to pushback, causing us to backtrack in order to bring people up to speed. I believe a better approach is to bring them along by going through the four phases.

The time it takes to go through these stages can vary depending on the severity of the problem. Sometimes it can be very short; for instance, in an emergency situation, we go from unawareness to action almost instantly. If it's strategic, it takes more time. Constant communication at all times is critical to success and building credibility as an effective manager and, more importantly, as a good leader.

HABIT 49

CREATE VALUE FIRST AND REWARD WILL FOLLOW

"The only way to do great work is to love what you do." | Steve Jobs

As I mentioned, the first real job I had was a production supervisor in an electronics manufacturing plant of the Ford Motor company on the midnight shift. Even though I had a bright, shiny, new engineering degree, I felt buried in a large corporate entity—out of sight and out of mind. This was not good enough for me. I had dreams of considerable proportions and I wanted my reward for my years of study <u>now</u>, not later!

After several months, I decided that nobody was going to reward me for simply being another supervisor on the midnight shift. I needed to do something to create value right away and get noticed. So, without being asked, I taught myself to use database software, started collecting quality information on a certain manufacturing line, and generated suggested improvements for quality and efficiency. Soon afterward, I was noticed and moved to supervise a new production line on the afternoon shift. Again, I developed the habit of creating value first, and shortly afterward I was given more responsibilities and promoted to a day shift job and, ultimately, greater management roles. I developed the habit of doing more than I was paid to do.

To develop the habit of doing more than you are paid to do, take the following actions:

- Take initiative. Do not wait to be told what to do next.

- Seek opportunities for high-impact improvements that generate a significant value with minimal resources.

- Don't broadcast what you are doing before you get results. Get started, get results and then promote yourself, as the results will give you credibility.

- Change your mindset and get used to working for free, which in reality is deferred payment. This is how entrepreneurs think.

It takes a lot of faith to believe that results will eventually follow your actions and that you will be rewarded for the effort. Often, the reward is impossible to detect or it comes much later than expected. However, if you maintain the faith that it will happen, over time, your belief will grow stronger and your rewards will be greater.

HABIT 50

LEARN TO SELL

"Remember, people don't buy for logical reasons. They buy for emotional reasons." | Zig Ziglar

Every single person needs to know how to sell. If you doubt me, consider the following situations:

The child wants cookies, so she needs to sell her parents and convince them to give her cookies. The sales pitch is usually pointing at the cookie jar, screaming to get attention (constant promotion) and not stopping until she gets the cookie (closing)!

A young man is interested in a young woman and he needs to sell her on dating him. The sales pitch is him listing the benefits she'd receive by dating him (promotes the benefits, not the features), as he showers her with attention and demonstrates how he is unique, relative to the competition (unique selling proposition).

A student decides to go to art school rather than engineering school and needs to sell his parents on the merits of funding his university experience. The sales pitch is finding their pain point (not wanting an uneducated kid living at home requiring constant care and attention), proposing a solution (schooling) and the parents agreeing to fund tuition (the close).

Learning how to sell your ideas to other people is a fundamental skill that's critical to personal and professional success. People who strive to achieve extraordinary levels of success must learn to sell their ideas with passion, vigor and confidence in order to gain cooperation. The result will be that people will help us achieve our big goals and, in the process, help themselves.

The *10 Critical Steps* necessary to effective selling are:

1. Sell yourself first so you are committed to your product or service.

2. Focus on solving a problem or relieving a pain.

3. Focus on helping create value, save time, reduce risk or make money.

4. Build rapport and trust. People buy from people they like.

5. Find the emotional reason people will buy, justified with logic.

6. Practice handling objections.

7. A.B.C. (Always Be Closing).

8. Learn how to handle rejection and never take no for an answer.

9. Use a system that supports your sales effort.

10. Never quit.

HABIT 51

BE AN EXCEPTIONAL LISTENER

"Better to remain silent and be thought a fool than to speak out and remove all doubt." | Abraham Lincoln

Most of us truly are poor listeners. Rather than listen, we often wait for a break in the conversation so we have our turn to talk.

By listening, you put yourself in a state of mind where you are open and receptive to new ideas. You are building personal rapport and giving yourself the opportunity to think. By listening, you put yourself in a service-oriented state of mind where you can learn something.

Listening is an important leadership skill, as it creates understanding, empathy and critical thinking skills. It gives you the opportunity to understand the speaker's problems, which helps you be more creative in servicing their problems and ultimately gaining their support. Listening is a great way to demonstrate to others that you care deeply about them. This is important not only in personal relationships but also in business. Finally, listening is the best way to help keep your emotions in check, particularly during crucial conversations or stressful and emotional situations, where you risk saying something inappropriate. In these situations, listening gives you the opportunity to cool off a bit, and become more thoughtful.

I have found that the three most important ways to improve listening skills are the following:

Focus 100% on the Speaker. When someone is speaking to you, don't try to multitask, check your email or flip through papers; stop everything and listen intently to what he or she has to say. Look him or her in the eye, stop all other activities and focus on the speaker.

If You Don't Understand Something, Ask a Question. Don't interject or try to paraphrase, but rather ask questions that give the other person the opportunity to respond respectively, openly and clearly. By asking the speaker to clarify, you can also help guide the conversation in a way that helps you understand what is most important.

Use Respectful Body Language. When you're listening, don't sit with your legs crossed, your arms folded and a big scowl on your face. This tells the speaker that you don't care what they have to say, and that you're only waiting for your chance to speak. Take the time to open your body and use appropriate body language. Face the speaker, not directly head-on or in a confrontational way, but in a relaxed, calm and non-threatening way. *Be aware of your body language, as it usually communicates more than your words.*

HABIT 52

ASK QUALITY QUESTIONS TO GET QUALITY INFORMATION

*"Judge a man by his questions
rather than his answers."* | Voltaire

Great leaders develop a habit of learning about other people. They seek out information about their qualities, motivation and inspiration, and use that information to help them accomplish goals. They do this by developing the habit of asking quality questions.

Some leaders fall into the trap of being a one-way communicator; they dictate information instead of exchanging it. That's not a leader, it's a manager or a boss! A leader is engaged in constant, two-way conversation with the people who work for and with him or her. A leader influences people to move in a certain direction, to be inspired, to be their best and to achieve their goals.

You can use this technique to influence people while exchanging information. You may ask questions when you sincerely lack information and need to understand. However, if you already have all the necessary information, asking these questions can lead the speaker through their own process of self-understanding. By asking a series of quality questions, you can help clarify someone else's thinking.

Exceptional leaders are like world-class interviewers. If you look at the best in the world, who rose to the top of their game, they rarely dictate their point of view. They bring out the views of others through a series of quality questions.

What is a quality question?

It's thoughtful. Don't blurt out the first thing that pops into your head.

It's short. Get to the point swiftly.

It's open-ended. A closed-ended question is often seen as being arrogant or manipulative.

It's respectful. A quality question leaves the person feeling good about the interaction.

I'm not suggesting one should go through leadership roles only asking questions, as different situations require different kinds of communications. However, asking quality questions—questions that inspire, clarify and help build relationships—is an important habit for a leader.

HABIT 53

SEEK FIRST TO UNDERSTAND AND THEN TO BE UNDERSTOOD

"You can close more business in two months by being interested in other people than you can in two years by trying to get people interested in you." | Dale Carnegie

Leaders often struggle with getting their messages out, and therefore can be frequently misunderstood or ignored. A leader needs to seek to understand first, and then to be understood.

By better understanding the circumstances, a leader can truly understand a problem, and a team can solve the problem. Understanding is a critical step in building the habit of great leadership over time. *Avoid overreacting, as situations often deteriorate through a lack of information and poor communications coupled with immediate reactions.* You must first take a step back to be more thoughtful about a situation.

When you seek to understand first and then to be understood, you put the responsibility back on yourself to make sure you have all the information necessary at that time to make a decision. By developing this habit of seeking to understand and then to be understood, people become more effective leaders and better communicators.

Consider the following tips:

Put the Person in a More Relaxed State of Mind. They may be feeling defensive or emotional; therefore, work to neutralize these before you try to put people in a different state.

Reflect on the Other Person's Perspective. Pause momentarily and genuinely focus on the other person while making a sincere effort to view the problem or communications from his or her perspective.

Avoid Critical Conversations When You Don't Have Sufficient Time or Information. This is particularly important if you are in a rush, distracted or working with partial information. Find the right time to have the conversation.

Keep an Open Mind. Your goal should be to fully understand another's perspective before you try to change it. First, ask a series of questions, then contemplate what the other person is saying, and then take a moment to clarify and articulate your own point of view.

HABIT 54

BECOME A VALUE-ADDED NETWORKER

"Stop Selling. Start Helping." | Zig Ziglar

We live in a world where it has never been easier to stay connected, so developing the habit of becoming a *value-added networker* is critically important as you build your career, family and business.

There is truly not enough time to learn all the skills, access all the resources, gain all the insights and make all the mistakes necessary to achieve our goals. There is not enough runway, so we need the help and cooperation of others. The people who will help us the most are the ones who stand to gain or benefit from our own experiences; they will help us along the way in direct proportion to the amount of help we can provide them. This, in its simplest form, is the *value-added network.*

A network is not a group of people on standby for your call so they can help you. It is the collective experience of the people around you who are looking to gain from their association with you.

Building a great network starts with mindset. Every day, think about what you can do to improve your networking skills and network.

179

It needs to be on your mind during all your regular interactions throughout the day.

Focus on what you can do for people, not what people can do for you, and how you can both benefit from the interaction.

You need to provide value to your network, even if it's simply calling to say hello or to get to know someone better. Or perhaps it's to provide a small amount of information, connect in some way, or help them and their family. Whatever it is, every interaction has to make that person connect with you in a slightly stronger way; by making him or her a little bit better, he or she will be happy to return it to you tenfold.

You need to have the mechanics in place. Keep a system that organizes all the people in your network, and then use that system to call people—not when you need them, but when you don't need them. Call or connect with people frequently. You should be calling the key contacts in your network once a year, even if it is to wish them a happy birthday, Merry Christmas or a good start to the year.

Treat each person you meet as a potential addition to your network. If you feel that you have mutual interest, then add him or her to your database and make a point of connecting regularly.

There are many great references on how to network. My favorite is *Never Eat Alone* (Crown Publishing Group, 2005) by Ken Ferazzi and Tahl Raz.

If you do these things, you will build a valuable network over your lifetime, a network that will be there on the days you do need it. Maintain the mindset that it's important to connect with people in meaningful, lasting ways. *Don't hesitate a moment—start today!*

MOVE FROM NOVICE TO EXPERT

"An expert is someone who has succeeded in making decisions and judgments simpler through knowing what to pay attention to and what to ignore." | Edward De Bono

In a 1982 article by Patricia Benner, called *From Novice to Expert*, she describes the five levels of competency and the leadership attributes of each level. The levels are novice, advanced beginner, competent, proficient, and expert. While the article was written in the context of nursing leadership, it applies to all forms of leadership.

Benner's description of expert performance is excellent. She states:

At the expert level, the performer no longer relies on an analytical principle (rule, guideline or maxim) to connect her/ his understanding of the situation to appropriate action. The expert...has an intuitive grasp of the situation and zeroes in on the accurate region of the problem without wasteful consideration of a large range of unfruitful possible problem situations. It is very frustrating to try to capture verbal descriptions of expert performance because the expert operates from a deep understanding of the situation, much like a chess master who, when asked why he made a particularly masterful move, will just say, "Because it felt right. It looked good."

181

This description is very consistent with the business experts I have known over the years, particularly those with a highly developed emotional intelligence and deep reservoirs of knowledge based on many years of experience. They trust their instincts and are able to make great decisions with fragments of information.

This raises two very big questions for a business leader, owner or entrepreneur: **Where am I on the novice to expert scale? What am I doing now to move to the expert level?**

If you are getting started in your career, or even in the first 10 to 15 years of your career, you still have much to learn, as you likely don't know what you don't know. If you are much further into your career, you still likely have much to learn, but at least you will know what you don't know. Be honest with yourself and assess where you are. Get third-party assessments, and be open to feedback about your skill level from mentors and coaches. Be realistic and pragmatic about your competency, particularly if you are relatively new to a field or profession.

If you want to move up the proficiency scale, do the following:

- Dedicate yourself to a lifelong program of personal development and continuous improvement. Read good books, take courses and build good habits.

- Find a *Mastermind* (See Habit 67 for more information about a *Mastermind*), group, coach or mentor that will help you accelerate your improvement and teach you.

- Get as much experience as possible and embrace the difficulties in order to accelerate growth, so you can make mistakes, learn and get there faster.

The 'intuitive grasp of the situation' that Benner believes defines an expert comes with time, difficulty and practice. *It comes from staying in the game, from sticking to one profession, industry or area of focus, and from persevering in the face of great hardships.* This is how champions are made, and over time, you too will move from a novice to an expert.

ACTIONS FOR TRACTION

What leadership skills do you admire most in a leader?

_____

_____

_____

What leadership skills do you need to develop to be more successful?

_____

_____

_____

What are the three most important listening skills, and how can you incorporate them into your next conversation?

_____

_____

_____

Who would you like to add to your network and how can you make it happen?

_____

_____

_____

CHAPTER 9

COMMUNICATING WITH POISE

"Think like a wise man but communicate in the language of the people." | William Butler Yeats

MY STORY: IT SEEMED LIKE A GOOD IDEA AT THE TIME

As my career has progressed, developing the ability to communicate well has always been a priority. Being born in Ireland gave me natural advantages, as communications is an important part of the Irish culture. Now, well into my corporate career, I was learning about the profound relationship between communications and leadership. Through trial and error, and lots of it, I was learning that communicating is a critical soft skill and an expression of character. Little did I know how important it would be in the next phase of my career.

My transition from a general management role to executive leadership took place after I left Pirelli Cables and joined Ballard Power Systems in the late 1990s. One of my main responsibilities with Ballard was to work closely with our partner Daimler-Benz, in Stuttgart, Germany. I spent much time in Germany during the years I was with Ballard and developed good relationships with my counterparts there. The fact that I was born in Europe helped. I also had a technical background and had run a manufacturing business, which also gave me some credibility. Finally, and I believe most importantly, having previously worked for both an American and an Italian company, I understood cultural differences and, specifically, how to work closely with many people in a cooperative way across multiple cultures in order to get things done.

Several years after having joined Ballard, I was required to visit our subsidiary in a little town outside Stuttgart, to make an important announcement. Knowing how critical this communication was, I decided that I needed to do something different to demonstrate our commitment to our employees and partners, and to bridge the divide between the Canadian and German cultures.

To do this effectively, I got this idea into my head that I would give my speech in German, even though I hardly knew a word of the language! I was looking for a way to connect more deeply. I wrote out a very brief speech in English, about a half page long, and then spent a couple of hours with my local German manager who helped translate it and then gave me a fast phonetics tutorial on how to deliver it in German. We rehearsed several times in a conference room, and since it was only the two of us, the atmosphere was relaxed.

I was far less relaxed two hours later, as I stood in front of several hundred Germans, including a number of important officials from Daimler-Benz. The original idea of giving this particular speech in German now seemed far less appealing than it had a few hours earlier. I had never learned another language, and now, in my infinite wisdom, I had decided to give an important announcement in German!

Nevertheless, I knew how communications and leadership are intertwined, and I was determined to go ahead and do the best that I possibly could. I approached the lectern, opened my notes and proceeded. "Mein name ist Eamonn Percy," I said, which means "My name is Eamonn Percy." I proceeded to the next line of my speech, saying how happy I was to be here. I was struggling through the third line when suddenly the audience broke into spontaneous applause. I was stunned. Even though I was clearly in way over my head, the audience was actually appreciating the fact that I was making the effort to speak their language. The ice had been broken and I quickly wrapped up the last few lines. I had shown my vulnerabilities and my weaknesses, but I had also showed my nature, demonstrating that I really did care and that I wanted to connect at a deeper level.

This experience stuck with me for the rest of my career as I went through other roles and started building my own business. In the end, I realized that good communication is not only about what you say or even how you say it—it is really about how people feel after you say what needs to be said. It can define the quality of your leadership and your courage. It's rarely what you say or your choice of words. Instead, it is your empathy, the feelings that go into your words, the caring, the listening, the body language and the heart that make a difference and that separate good communicators from great ones.

This brief experience in connecting with people across a different culture and a foreign language showed me that good communication is universally understood. It showed me that we all can make differences in our lives and in the lives of many others if we learn to communicate well. It showed me that communication is ultimately a demonstration of our character and our resilience, and how much we care for our fellow human beings.

HABIT 56

LEVERAGE BODY LANGUAGE

"What you do speaks so loud that I cannot hear what you say." | Ralph Waldo Emerson

Every great leader must be keenly attuned to body language: their own, their peers and that of the people they are leading. Our words only convey part of the message: the tone of our words and body language are more important.

Body language is how people broadcast their inner emotions in non-verbal terms. Understanding it is incredibly useful, as it can help you gain insight into how the people around you feel.

How do you develop the habit of using body language to become a better leader?

Be Observant. Look at the way people sit, their facial expressions, and the way that they carry themselves. These small actions broadcast their emotions and their intentions.

Be Inquisitive. Be curious about what people are thinking, how they feel and their emotions. Try to view yourself from someone else's perspective to understand how you react to certain situations and how your body broadcasts your reaction.

Learn to Alter Your Own Body Language. By forcing a smile, you'll find that you actually do feel happier. If you start to feel better, those around you will feel better too. If someone's body language is preventing you from communicating effectively, try changing your own. Stand up, move around or take on a more relaxed posture. Open your posture, unfold your arms and lean forward. If you're interested in something someone has to say, look him or her directly in the eye. These little changes in your own body language will help improve your state, which will also help you change the state of others.

To improve your own state by giving yourself more confidence, try these body language movements as described in the book, *The Silent Language of Leaders* (Wiley, 2011) by Carol Kinsey Goman:

- To boost your confidence, assume a power pose.

- To increase participation, look like you're listening.

- To encourage collaboration, remove barriers.

- To connect instantly with someone, shake hands.

- To stimulate good feelings, smile.

- To show agreement, mirror expressions and postures.

- To improve your speech, use your hands.

- If you want to know the truth, watch people's feet.

- To sound authoritative, keep your voice down.

- And to improve your memory, uncross your arms and legs.

HABIT 57

BE AN EXPERT IN HANDLING CRUCIAL CONVERSATIONS

"A coach is someone who can give correction without causing resentment." | Coach John Wooden

Have you ever had the experience of saying something, and then, as the words were leaving your lips, you knew you would regret it? Ouch. This tends to occur when we are discussing a particularly important or emotional topic, or if we are under stress, pressed for time, or with people who are important to us.

After character development, effective communications is one of the most important skills a leader needs to develop. *In fact, I believe that empathy, which is key to character development, is also the foundation of all effective communication.* While learning how to communicate as a leader at all times is important, knowing how to communicate during a crucial conversation is *most important.* People may overlook a faux pas when the stakes are low, but will find it unforgivable when stakes are high, egos are in overdrive and emotions are in the danger zone. Great leaders tread carefully and thoughtfully during these times.

While crucial conversations represent a small percentage of our conversational time, they can largely define our relationship with others. They are the conversations that can make or break a leader, and can establish a reputation that soars to great heights or flounders in mediocrity. These conversations are usually defined by a heightened degree of importance, risk and vulnerability to both parties, for example, a conversation with an employee over poor performance, demotion, or denial of an opportunity; a conversation with a spouse concerning significant parenting issues; or a conversation with a business partner or workmate about a work relationship problem.

Becoming skilled in handling critical conversations will help you build cooperative and rewarding relationships, and trust, with people you care about most while you build your leadership muscle.

Try the following:

Collect Your Thoughts. Take a moment to reflect on what you are going to say and how you are going to say it.

Lead with the Truth. It is always easier to be empathetic and genuine when you speak plainly and truthfully. While people may not *like* to hear it, they will certainly appreciate your candor and *respect* you for it.

Be Authentic. Don't try to be anyone but yourself. Speak from the heart, in your own words, and in your own way, demonstrating both courage and sincerity.

Pace Yourself. If emotions are running high, literally take a deep breath and slow down. While it may seem like an eternity to you, the pause in the conversation will seem normal and helpful.

Get Perspective. View the conversation from the other person's perspective. Under stress, we develop tunnel vision as we become determined to get through our script. Try to look at the situation from the other person's perspective and understand his or her emotional state.

Avoid Full-Stop Words. At all costs, avoid any emotionally laden words or phrases that can explode the conversation quickly and bring it to a quick stop, such as "you should," "you always," or particularly descriptive negative words. Speak the way you would like to be spoken to.

Be Brief. Get right to the point early in the conversation and avoid a big buildup. You should have made your main point within the first minute, if not the first 30 seconds.

Focus on the Issue, Not the Person. Leaders build up people on their strengths, not weaknesses. When people feel attacked, they become defensive and resistant to change.

Don't Bring Up Multiple Issues. Deal with one issue at a time to avoid a conversation getting overly complex and out of control. Avoid trying to deal with multiple grievances simultaneously. Respectfully defer other topics to a later time.

Say What Needs to Be Said and Then Move On. Focus on the quality of the conversation, not the quantity. Don't let the conversation degrade to a marathon session that will bring up tangential issues and cause more problems for the future.

No matter what happens or how poorly you feel you did, don't brood or dwell on your performance. Handle the conversation as well as you possibly can and then move on. Self-doubt will erode your own confidence and lessen your effectiveness in the future. Having done your best, let it stand!

HABIT 58

CHOOSE YOUR WORDS CAREFULLY

*"Teach thy tongue to say, "I do not know," and
thou shalt progress."* | Maimonides

We are filled with human emotions like pride, jealousy, envy and fear.
As a result, we can react emotionally to words that other people use
to describe us or our behavior.

Words have different meanings to different people. Over time, a
word comes to mean more than its dictionary definition and gains
new meanings based on our previous experiences, biases, beliefs or
values. We are particularly sensitive to words directed at us personally
or at our appearance, intelligence or family.

Under stress, we tend to revert back to our core personality, which can
bring out the worst in the way we express ourselves. If not properly
controlled, this behavior can have negative long-term effects on our
closest relationships.

The use of cruel or harsh words is like a nail being driven into a piece
of wood. It does a lot of damage on the way in, and it leaves a mark
even after it is pulled out.

Take time to choose your words carefully by doing the following:

Always De-escalate. We usually blurt out something we regret when we are in a highly emotional, stressful or agitated state. Think de-escalation and have the maturity to be the person who steps back from the situation before it gets out of hand. Prevention is the best medicine.

Avoid Personal Attacks, even if you feel, or know, they are justified. Do this by staying focused on the issue at hand, not the person. By constantly focusing on the issue, no matter how ridiculous the other person is being, you will not be baited into a confrontation.

Mentally Count to Three. My mother used this on me when I was a young boy (though in my case, she needed to count to 10). It gave her a mini cooling-off period and it gave me a chance to smarten up, ultimately allowing everyone to gain some composure.

Improve Your Vocabulary so you have the right word for the right occasion. The person you're dealing with might even be temporarily stunned by your choice of words, in awe or confusion. At a minimum, you will have the right word for the circumstances and avoid any confusion created by a poor vocabulary.

Breathe Deeply and Slowly during critical conversations. It will help you stay calm and relaxed.

Be a person of character, and someone that makes a positive difference in the lives of people around you. Lead with your strong character by taking the time to be respectful and considerate, both in thoughts and actions. Words have important meaning, and in many cases, strong meaning. Be a leader by choosing them carefully.

HABIT 59

COMMUNICATE TO INFLUENCE AND INFORM

"When dealing with people, remember you are not dealing with creatures of logic, but with creatures of emotion, creatures bristling with prejudice, and motivated by pride and vanity." | Dale Carnegie

When I want to illustrate that we humans are creatures of emotion and not logic, I conduct a simple demonstration. I ask someone to face me and to place their hand in the air, with the palm forward. I then gently place the palm of my hand on their hand without any pressure. After a few seconds, and without saying a word, I apply a very light pressure forward onto their palm. Immediately, the person applies some pressure back to resist. I slightly increase the pressure, and they start pushing back harder. Within a few moments, I am applying my full force on their hand and they are pushing back with full force. I never asked the person to push back nor to hold their hand in place. I normally stop the demonstration here before it descends into a full-blown shoving match. *However, the point is made: people instinctively push back.*

I have conducted this demonstration a number of times and have yet to have a single person allow me to push their hand forward more than a few inches. In every case, big or small, male or female, people have pushed back. I use this to demonstrate a key point about communications and leadership: most humans, out of biological and evolutionary necessity, are hardwired to push back, to resist, to defend their position. We are not starting from a neutral or receptive position, rather one of instinctive resistance.

Ignore this insight to human behavior, and you risk a long and perilous road as an effective communicator. Embrace it, and you will have the ability to get virtually anything done.

Being an effective communicator is not about informing; instead, it's about influencing behaviors. With the obvious exceptions of an emergency situation, simple tasks, transferring hard data or hierarchical situations, effective communication is about persuading and influencing people. Rarely is it about transferring information.

Communicating to influence encourages sharpened interpersonal skills, develops greater relationship bonds and helps create long-term trust. It broadcasts that you care and are genuinely interested in a person's well-being by being an advocate for a strong position. It communicates with a sense of respect for the relationship.

Here are the five actions you can take to communicate with influence:

Neutralize First. Start a conversation by reducing instinctive resistance. Put the person in a neutral state. Do this by being authentic and transparent upfront, showing respect, and framing the conversation appropriately. If they start to push back, avoid the temptation to push back harder; instead, be flexible and understanding, but firm.

Provide Context. Most people are willing and eager to help but often resist out of pride and lack of information. Ease this risk by providing some context for communications before you get into the heart of the matter. Don't assume people know all that you know.

Choose Your Timing. It's hard to influence anyone when they are completely distracted or worried about something bigger than your problems. Be thoughtful about the time, place and method of your communication, so you give the other person the maximum opportunity to successfully engage you.

Understand Their World. Influencers take the time to understand the other person's world, then communicate in terms they can relate to. Be sincere, be clear and communicate in a way that is understood.

Focus on a Goal. Never forget that the objective of communication is to make something happen, so stay focused on the specific action you want to happen next. Confirm this understanding and seek a commitment, or pledge, from the other person. Always double-check the understanding in clear and simple language.

HABIT 60

DELIVER BAD NEWS WITH GRACE AND DIGNITY

"Success is never final, failure is never fatal. It's courage that counts." | Coach John Wooden

Bad news is, unfortunately, part of life. Whether you are a business owner, employee, manager, parent or student, eventually you are going to have to deliver some bad news to someone.

For instance, as a business owner, you are faced with sharing bad news with employees, customers and others in your business; it comes with the territory.

Try the following process for delivering bad news:

Get All the Facts First. Go to primary sources, if possible, for the facts. Do not even consider relaying bad news unless you are 100% sure of the facts.

Prepare. Assemble your thoughts, plan your approach, print a script and practice if necessary. Do whatever is required to ensure you are properly prepared.

Provide Context. Provide the recipients of the bad news with some context so they understand the information in a broader perspective, and know that you have been thoughtful in your approach.

Be Courageous and Brief. Drum up the courage and say what needs to be said. Do not delay and avoid a convoluted, watered-down half-truth. Be courageous, be brief and be gone.

Engage. Ask the person if he or she has any questions, needs clarification or has any comments. Provide an opportunity to engage, but do not overdo it—the person may need some time to absorb it himself or herself!

HABIT 61

MASTER WRITING GREAT SPEECHES

"The most important things are the hardest to say because words diminish them." | Stephen King

Throughout your life, you will likely be called upon to say a few words at an event or to give a formal speech. Sometimes these opportunities to speak are impromptu, requiring you to think on your feet, while on other occasions you will have more time to prepare. This is a critical moment in your journey and it's something you need to know how to handle.

Public speaking is the chance to leverage your skills and experience in order to make a meaningful impact on a large number of people. It can also enhance your personal brand, move you closer to the achievement of your goals, and bring greater opportunity and prosperity by demonstrating your skills and values.

Short Speech: (less than two minutes)

If time is short and you are asked to say a few important words, do the following:

- Create a **Thank You Sandwich**. (Start with **Thank You**, make your comments, and end with **Thank You**.)

- Be exceedingly brief and to the point.

- Stick with one core idea that is memorable.

- Be authentic.

Longer Speech:

If you have more time to prepare a speech, then do the following:

- Prepare an audience analysis by gathering as much information as possible, so you can tailor your comments.

- Create an outline of your speech—with a clear beginning, middle and summary—on several key points.

- Write the entire speech in advance and in bullet point form.

- Make it memorable with personal anecdotes, illustrations, examples and statistics.

- End with a call to action or a net effect goal, so your audience has a value-added takeaway.

- Practice it several times in advance, and record yourself for additional scrutiny and feedback.

For more information on how to prepare and deliver a great speech, see the *Recommended Additional Resources* at the end of the book.

HABIT 62

BE A PUBLIC SPEAKING PRO

"Wise men talk because they have something to say; fools because they have to say something." | Plato

Numerous studies indicate that people fear public speaking more than death. Imagine, many people would rather be quiet and dead than alive and speaking in public! I think this is largely a result of ignorance of how fun and easy it is to be a public speaker. I have given many public speeches over my career, and can assure you that it is a pleasant and enriching experience.

Sure, it takes some courage to get over your fear, and yes, it takes practice to be good at it. However, if you are starting out, I can guarantee you that <u>any</u> audience will be exceedingly supportive of someone who is genuinely making the effort. If anything, it will make you feel more alive, and the more you practice the better you will feel.

Developing the habit of speaking like a pro will give you confidence both on and off the stage, and give you a chance to make a meaningful difference in the world as you communicate your ideas with poise and style.

Public speaking is a learned skill, no different than learning to swim or ride a bike. There are simple steps you can take to build those skills and deliver your message in a way that counts.

When delivering your message, do the following:

Prepare. Never wing it; prepare or don't speak. Solid preparation is the most important aspect of giving a great talk. The bigger the audience, event and subject, the more preparation is necessary. Preparation can be as simple as jotting down bullet points, or as complex as a written speech. The process of preparing will make you more focused and confident with the material.

Focus on the Audience. Tell the audience members what they need to hear, not what you want to say. Take time to do a proper audience analysis by gathering information on the audience makeup (age, income levels, interests, etc.) and talk about what is important to them, not you. Be a blast, not a bore!

Set a Goal. Build your talk around the accomplishment of a goal. Don't speak to share information or to get something off your chest. Speak to persuade people into some action, a specific and worthy goal. It could be to support a cause, donate money, make a purchase or improve their own lives.

Have Fun. Let all fear go and focus on the occasion. Make it enjoyable and fun for both you and your audience. Smile and the audience will smile back. Use your body language and tone of voice to let them know that you care about them, and that being here, delivering this speech, is the only place you want to be right now.

Breathe Properly. Controlled breathing is the key to effective public speaking. Take two to three deep breaths before you go on stage, and concentrate on breathing slowly and deeply. This will relax you and help you concentrate. Continue to focus on taking long, deep breaths during your talk.

Use Your Body Well. Keep your body language relaxed but animated. Do not grip the lectern with white knuckles. Keep your hands out of your pockets. Move around the stage naturally, and you will engage an audience with your style, keeping their eyes focused on you and your subject, not the clock!

Use Your Voice. Practice moderating your voice so it sounds interesting and engaging. You can do this by recording your own voice and listening back later, or even by practicing in front of a mirror or family and friends. Do not be boring and do not speak in a monotone.

Be Enthusiastic. Show a high degree of enthusiasm for the subject, audience and yourself. People will know if you love the topic and enjoy giving the talk. Enthusiasm is highly infectious, so let it rip and have a great time. Both you and the audience will love it!

HARNESS THE POWER OF SILENCE

*"Speak only if it improves upon
the silence."* | Mahatma Gandhi

Nature abhors a vacuum and people abhor silence in a conversation. If we don't fill in every microsecond of the conversation with sounds, we are accused of creating an awkward silence or asked if 'the cat got your tongue' or, even worse, made to feel like we can't think of anything intelligent to say.

Don't fall into this communications trap. Remember, the fundamental rule of communication is to persuade, so only speak if you have something important to say.

Silence is often overlooked as a key part of communications. Effective communicators use every tool at their disposal in order to achieve their objective. In business, those objectives are to inspire action, persuade, motivate or sell. Silence can be an effective weapon in achieving any of those objectives.

If you are over-talking in a conversation, you may be putting yourself at risk, since you divulge more information the longer you talk. Additionally, you may be indicating your lack of knowledge when you are trying to build credibility, weakening yourself further at a time when you need credibility the most. Even the simple fact of talking means you are not listening at that moment and are therefore not learning.

Silence can be very effective if used in the following ways:

Pause in a Conversation if You Want to Make a Dramatic Point. Even a second or two of silence after a strong fact is presented will carry more weight with the listener then just a steady stream of words without emphasis.

In Negotiations, Keep Silent if Your Opponent Is Very Talkative. This is particularly important if they are nervous, as they will continue to spill the beans by revealing information or lack of knowledge.

Stay Silent After Listening to an Offer. If you remain silent after an offer has been made to you, the other person will likely read it as disapproval, disinterest or disgust. If you have the courage to stay silent long enough, they may make another better offer just to fill the awkward silence.

Use Silence to Broadcast the Gravity of a Situation. Often people let their imaginations run wild in the void of silence.

Use Silence to Show Your Appreciation for Someone or Their Work. There are moments when words truly cannot describe a situation. If you remain silent, your respect and admiration will come through louder than any words could.

ACTIONS FOR TRACTION

What are the three critical things to remember when having a crucial conversation?

_____

_____

_____

Practice delivering a two-minute speech.

_____

_____

_____

What is the one communication skill that is holding you back from significant achievement, and how can you improve it daily?

_____

_____

_____

How can you use silence to your advantage in a conversation?

_____

_____

_____

CHAPTER 10
GETTING THINGS DONE

*"Do what you can, where you are, with
what you have."* | Theodore Roosevelt

MY STORY: LEAVING A SAFE HARBOR

Ultimately, achievement, personal success and accomplishing big goals come down to one thing—getting things done! Thinking, planning, analyzing or reviewing all support getting things done, but are not actually doing the critical task. Getting things done is the critical event. Your goal each day is to do. Thinking is important, but the goal is to become a doer, not just a thinker.

I have been known throughout my corporate career as the guy who got things done. I was called The Operations Guy, The Operator and even The Executioner one time due to my relentless focus on execution—of tasks, not people! However, I never really deeply appreciated how important this was until I permanently left the corporate world and set out to build my own business.

My transition from the corporate world to the entrepreneurial world, from being an employee to being a business owner, was both exciting and daunting. I was giving up a lot of positives from the corporate world, such as a lucrative executive salary, bonuses, personal prestige, a nice office and support staff. However, I was also giving up office politics, pointless meetings, petty jealousy, a poor health lifestyle and an income cap.

What was I gaining with this transition? An uncertain future, a difficult road ahead, raw exposure of my weaknesses and a test of my own ability to create value in the marketplace. I was gaining the potential to generate economic freedom for myself and my family, now and for many generations to come.

As a corporate executive, profound weaknesses holding one back from exceptional growth and performance are rarely discussed in depth. There is a tendency to gloss over or discuss weaknesses superficially, since the risks of exposing weaknesses far outweigh the benefits. There may be an annual performance review with corresponding recommendations for employee development or areas that 'need improvement.' However, the world of an entrepreneur is more raw and, quite frankly, helpful. Personal weaknesses show up on your cash flow statement as lost opportunity or a canceled contract, not as a line item on an annual performance review. Customers give the feedback, not your boss. Over time, if unaddressed, personal weaknesses can turn into material flaws that may ultimately sink your business and change the economic prospects of your family. Entrepreneurs have a huge incentive to understand weaknesses and fix them fast!

To succeed as a business owner, I am required to address my weaknesses head-on, every day. I am required to put even more discipline into my life and my business, to focus intently on the skills and habits necessary to get things done and create value. Personally, I realize that while I had been known as the guy who got things done, it was not enough. It was now up to me to get up, get going, and permanently slay any remaining poor disciplines.

I started looking for a good system to help me improve these disciplines and make me a better entrepreneur and business owner. I read a number of books on the topic (see *Additional Recommended Resources* for more information) and read through the materials from great authors, including Coach John Wooden, Napoleon Hill and Brian Tracy, but to no avail. I was looking for something very specific and exceedingly pragmatic, something I could literally use each and every day, like driving a car or using a phone.

One evening, I was reading through a biography of Benjamin Franklin, when I came upon exactly what I needed! Even though Benjamin Franklin was one of the leading American thinkers, inventors, statesmen and entrepreneurs, apparently even he struggled with daily discipline. Whether it was procrastination, disorganization, poor judgment, moral relapses or simply thinking wrong, even Franklin needed to be held accountable. He devised a system that he used and that immediately appealed to my sense of order and simplicity. Since he knew he could not trust himself 100% to do the right thing, at the right time, for the right reason each day, he started tracking his deviations from his code of conduct based on 13 moral principles. Each day he would mark down where he had failed to live up to this code and strive to do better the next day. He simply brought his minor lapses to his attention, each day! He didn't run from the problem; rather, he ran to it. I thought to myself, "If it worked for Benjamin Franklin, it must work for me." After all, he must have done something right for his image to end up on the US $100 bill!

I immediately started adopting his system and maintain it to this day. It is an eye-opener, to say the least. And if you are at all squeamish about exploring your own weaknesses, I suggest you NOT do it. However, if you really want to understand how you can take small daily mistakes, learn from them, forgive yourself and then get better, I suggest you give it a try. I expanded it to include certain health, wealth and exercise habits.

For more information on Franklin's system, go to *One Way to Permanently Change Habits* at the end of this book.

HABIT 64

FORGET MULTITASKING—FOCUS!

"Concentrate all your efforts upon the work at hand.
The sun's rays do not burn through until brought
into focus." | Alexander Graham Bell

We are inundated by numerous tasks throughout the day, big and small, important and non-important, urgent and non-urgent. Some are our own priorities, while many are the priorities of others. We can easily become overwhelmed by these tasks and risk becoming ineffective or stressed, and make mistakes. Many of these tasks contribute very little toward our achievement of big goals.

We naturally default to a system of managing tasks that is based on our past experience, and we often do not stop to reflect whether or not our multitasking is even effective. We tend to believe that multitasking is a good because we often confuse being busy with being effective. Multitasking gives the impression of momentum and activity, which can feed our need for accomplishment.

The digital distraction environment has made this phenomenon more pronounced. Between email, phone calls and other notifications, it becomes almost impossible to focus on a single task for more than a few minutes during a normal workday without closing the door and turning off the phone and computer.

I am here to break the news that you are likely a much less effective multitasker than you think. Recent neuroscience studies show a direct and significant correlation between increased distractions, largely from technology, and decreased concentration and academic performance. One study found that it can take an average of 15 minutes to return to a high level of concentration after a single distraction, such as a phone call. Another found that students who check Facebook even once in a 15-minute period (on average) have a poorer academic performance than their counterparts who don't check it as frequently.

Developing the habit of focusing on critical tasks is crucial to long-term success in business or any other profession. The ability to concentrate on one task over a prolonged period of time will give you a significant advantage over your competitors and greatly assist you in the achievement of your goals.

Here is how to stay focused:

Significantly Limit Technological Distractions in Your Life. Avoid excess social media, email, internet surfing and television. Consider checking email only once or twice a day, and turning off your smartphone during important periods of concentration.

Make It a Habit to Avoid Time-Consuming People and Activities. Don't allow other people to *interrupt you* if you need to seriously concentrate. This can be done by putting a Do Not Disturb sign on your door, which most people will respect. Schedule as if your life depended on it.

Acknowledge that You Are Likely Not a Multitasker. Take the time to understand your own particular ability to multitask. Do this by asking someone you know and trust for his or her insight. Alternatively, think about the times in your life when you have been very efficient and replicate those circumstances when required.

Develop Flow in Your Work by Focusing on One Task Until It Is Complete. Flow is a physiological state of deep immersion and focus on a singular task, where all other distractions disappear, and all emotion and concentration are directed toward the desired outcome. This state of flow will dramatically increase your productivity while helping you develop a good long-term habit.

HABIT 65

FOCUS ON RELENTLESS ACTION

"I have been impressed with the urgency of doing. Knowing is not enough; we must apply. Being willing is not enough; we must do." | Leonardo da Vinci

Some people seem to be perpetually winning, moving forward all the time, despite the fact that they may not have gone to the best school, or come from the 'right' circumstance or, quite frankly, even be that bright. These people seem to be able to attract success in an uncanny way; they are always doing the right things and moving in the right direction.

Others seem to languish. They have the right degrees, the right answers and all the trappings of success, but they really do not seem to achieve much. They talk a lot about achievement and seem to have an opinion about everything. However, behind the veneer, it is all talk!

Talk is cheap, while action is priceless. The difference is that while the talker is busy describing what he plans to do, the action taker is busy actually doing it. Nothing happens without action!

Action is like the fuel for a car. A car can have lots of potential energy, but it can only be turned into kinetic energy once fuel is added. Without fuel, it will sit there looking pretty for a while, but eventually, all the other cars will pass by and it will slowly rust away. *Action is the fuel of everyday living!*

Human beings are kinetic—we are literally built to move! Every fiber in our body, every sinew, every organ and every one of our senses is action-oriented, designed to make us live, move and achieve things. This is the natural state of affairs. Inaction goes against everything we are designed to do.

Relentless action may feel strange at first, particularly if you are overly concerned about the opinions of others. However, over time, becoming a person of action will align your mind and body. You will develop great energy and courage to spring forward, raising you to great heights of achievement, accomplishment and self-actualization.

Here is why I believe action is so important:

Action Creates Energy and Movement. Nothing else can move the needle to get you closer to your goal than action.

Action Overcomes Fear. You have probably heard the expression of being 'frozen by fear.' It is very true. If you have ever been in an emergency situation or under extreme pressure, there is a tendency to freeze up. Action, however small, releases us from that fear, gets our mind and body going, and moves us into a new and positive state.

Action Creates Momentum. It literally gets the ball rolling. Have you ever noticed how one little action can open up the floodgates? It can be a catalyst for doing something great. A well-placed phone call starts a sales process going. The road to financial freedom can start with signing up for one seminar. A weight loss program can start with a single walk around the block. Action gets things going.

Action Provides Feedback. You can theorize all day about the consequences of doing something, but you really don't know what will happen until you try. Say you want to buy your first home. You study all the right books and look at lots of listings. However, if you want to get a very quick and clear sense of buying a home, then take the action of making an offer. You may not get the home, but you can learn from it and try again, this time better informed and more experienced. You learn 80% of what you need to know the first time you do something, and then spend the rest of your life learning the other 20%.

Action Is Empowering. It literally moves the power from someone or something else to you. When you are being acted upon, you are out of control and can become a victim. By taking action, however small, you move the power back to yourself and regain control of your own destiny.

Action Is the Best Expression of Yourself. If you don't take action, the world, family, friends and external circumstances will define you, and you will not achieve your full human potential. Positive, enlightened and worthwhile action is the one way to show what you are truly made of, what you can accomplish and what you did during this short time we have on earth.

Here are 10 steps on how to become a *Relentless Action Taker*:

1. Make it a habit by taking daily, regular and consistent action.

2. For small decisions, don't overanalyze. Decide immediately and move on quickly.

3. For large decisions, set a deadline, make an action plan and start immediately.

4. Complete something each day that you have been putting off.

5. When very fearful, take an action, particularly one that requires physical movement to get started.

6. Avoid telling people what you plan to do. Impress with results, not talk.

7. If an action does not pan out, learn from it, correct your course and act again.

8. Focus your actions on high-value, productive activities, while avoiding time-consuming people and activities.

9. Don't confuse activity or being busy with productive action that moves you forward toward a worthwhile goal.

10. Avoid analysis paralysis. Gather sufficient information and then act.

HABIT 66

BE A PLAYER, NOT A SPECTATOR

"We can easily forgive a child who is afraid of the dark, the real tragedy of life is when men are afraid of the light." | Plato

My Grade 10 basketball coach, Mr. John Forsythe, used to tell me, one of the weaker players on the team, "Percy, just get in there and muck about." While it may not have been the strongest basketball coaching strategy, he did have a point. He knew that even a weak player in a good game environment has a better shot at success than he could ever get sitting on the bench just watching. It always made me feel like a player, not a spectator.

You need to be a player in the game of life, not a spectator watching the field. While you may have a game plan, the reality is that you'll spend most of your time in spontaneous action: driving the opportunity forward, jostling for position, holding back on pressure points, and working with your teammates to battle forward and achieve. These things only happen if you are in action on the field, not if you're on the bench or in the stands.

Even if your path is not 100% clear, or if you are fearful, uncertain, lacking resources, low in confidence or at a crossroads, the best path forward in life is to take action, get in there and be part of something. Nothing good will happen if you are waiting for the phone to ring, wasting time in a dead-end job, afraid to face your own potential. I believe that we all have a unique gift waiting to be unleashed and presented to the world. The best way to find that gift and achieve your potential is to jump into the game of life and keep being involved until a path forward emerges.

Here are the best ways to be a player, not a spectator:

Take Initiative. Be the person who starts first. This will help you build the skills necessary to execute well. Ultimately, people will start going to you naturally, reinforcing your status as a leader and bringing more opportunity your way.

Help More. If you have the time and interest, join a worthwhile organization and help. It gets you out there, meeting new groups of people and expanding your mind to new possibilities.

Be Bold. The more you rest, the more you rust. So take some bold initiatives that get you involved, preferably in a leadership role. For instance, rather than engaging in office gossip about the problems in your workplace, write a proposal to management suggesting improvements and offer to lead its implementation.

Don't Overanalyze—Act! Stop thinking so much! There is a time and place for thoughtful analysis. However, not every little move in your life needs to be thought through in detail. On a football team when the coach calls for offense, there are no committee meetings or philosophical conversations. The offensive team immediately runs onto the field and plays, period. Call your own offense!

Create Your Own Organization. If you don't see something immediately that you can jump into, create your own. Start a group, campaign, running club, investment club, parenting group, character building group or anything that appeals to you and gets you off the bleachers and into the game of life.

HABIT 67

UNLEASH THE POWER OF COOPERATION WITH A *MASTERMIND*

"Great things in business are never done by one person, they are done by a team of people." | Steve Jobs

In his exceptional book, *Think and Grow Rich*, Napoleon Hill introduced the concept of a *Mastermind* to the world. He spent 25 years studying more than 200 of the most successful people of his time to create principles of success. One of his principles was to create and leverage the power of a group of like-minded people—a *Mastermind. This is where the collective mental energy and capacity of a group of people could operate as 'one mind' in the achievement of a goal, in ways an individual could never accomplish.* He stated that no one can achieve his or her personal goals in complete isolation.

A *Mastermind* is an organized group of people who come together for a common purpose, where the collective thoughts of the group meld together in a new entity, to create new ideas and creativity that were not possible for any one individual in the group.

The *Mastermind* normally has a specific task to achieve, an obstacle to overcome or a goal to pursue. The group needs to meet regularly, have some organization, and develop high levels of trust in order to bond and create new, better ideas.

For instance, one could set up a *Mastermind* to help young professionals progress in their career, purchase real estate or invest together. It can be as simple as an organizing a Meetup or a breakfast club.

The key is to create a collective brain, which provides ideas and creativity well beyond what an individual could achieve.

Here are the key steps to forming and maintaining an effective *Mastermind*:

Make Your Intention 100% Clear. If you do not know exactly what it is that you are trying to achieve, you will never be able to attract the people around you necessary to achieve it. Be clear, be precise and be bold.

Let All Resistance Go. You can't move forward if your mind is in a state of fear or resistance. Let all thoughts of failure, fear and resistance go, and allow your mind to enter a state of openness.

Be Honest with Yourself. Have an honest conversation with yourself and recognize that you cannot do it in isolation. You need the help of others, particularly those with greater skills, experience and ability.

Take Action and Initiate. Form a group of people who will help you achieve your goal. They may be drawn from your personal or professional life.

Be Selective. Pick people in your *Mastermind* who fit your objective, bring complementary skill sets and are open to creative thinking. Allow zero room for negativity.

Harmonize Your Thoughts. A *Mastermind* is a single, harmonized virtual mind made up of multiple real minds. Focus the group on building and harmonizing a single thought, and then hold that in the forefront of your minds at all time.

HABIT 68

LEVERAGE THE POWER OF THE 80/20 RULE

"The key to success is to focus our conscious mind on things we desire, not things we fear." | Brian Tracy

In 1906 Italian economist Vilfredo Pareto discovered that 80% of the land in Italy was owned by 20% of the people. He conducted similar studies in other countries with similar results. Ironically, he also noticed the same principle applied to nature, as he discovered in his garden that only 20% of the pea pods contained 80% of the peas. In fact, unknowingly, he had stumbled upon an important universal principle *that 80% of the effect comes from approximately 20% of the causes.* This principle later became known as the *Pareto Principle*, in recognition of Vilfredo's contribution to its discovery.

This is a remarkably consistent law that exists in many aspects of our lives, for instance:

- The majority of the revenue from most companies comes from a minority of customers.

- The majority of the sales growth of a business tends to come from a very small number of products or services.

225

- Most of the personal wealth creation comes from a small number of sources (such as a principal residence, a pension, an investment or an owned business).

- About 80% of the successful projects in a company typically involve a small but highly productive group of people.

- Most of the taxes paid to the government come from a small percentage of the population. (According to *The Wall Street Journal*, in 2014, the top 20% of US income earners paid 84% of the taxes.)

Once you grasp this principle, it can become a very powerful tool in your toolkit to help you achieve greater results. You can control the vast majority of results in multiple aspects of your life by focusing your effort, and attention, on a small minority of the causes. To be effective, you need to consistently focus on the few actions that will bring you the greatest returns.

Putting the *Pareto Principle* into action:

Wealth. Make a list of all the actions that are most likely to create wealth, such as your job, investments, rental properties, businesses, pensions, etc. Prioritize the list, and then focus most of your effort on only the top one or two items. Over time, this strategy will give you the greatest possibility for wealth expansion.

Health. Make a list of the items that contribute most to a healthy lifestyle. The list will likely include: healthy eating, active living, low stress, proper sleep. Then make sure you focus your attention on the top one or two items.

Raising Children. There are only a few factors you can control that will have the biggest impact on a child's mental, emotional and physical health, for example, environment, the caregiver(s), schooling, sibling relationships and character development. Focus on doing these well and you will raise good children.

Generally, to leverage the *Pareto Principle*, make a list of all of the items contributing to your success and zero in on the one or two biggest contributors. Focus on those first. I am not suggesting that you ignore all the other factors, but that you recognize that you can make substantial improvement by focusing your effort on addressing the biggest factors first, and then, when you have achieved satisfactory results, move onto the next biggest factors.

HABIT 69

BUILD AN EXECUTION SYSTEM AND STICK TO IT

"A goal without a plan
is just a wish." | Antoine de Saint-Exupéry

W. Edward Deming was an American statistician credited with helping the Japanese become world leaders in manufacturing innovation and quality after World War II. He was largely ignored in the United States until near the end of his illustrious career.

In 1947, Deming started assisting Japanese manufacturers with the implementation of a system of business processes and strategies that enabled them to produce, and export, high-quality products to the rest of the world. His work was not appreciated in his home country of the US until 1981 when the Ford Motor Company recruited him as a consultant to help them develop their quality improvement initiatives of the 1980s. These initiatives were critical in reducing the competitive onslaught of Japanese automakers, and helped Ford and other US automakers become more successful.

I was fortunate to be working as an engineer with Ford in the 1980s and was trained in many of Deming's principles as part of a corporate-wide quality improvement training program. Our plant worked hard to put his principles into practical business practice. At the time, I did not fully appreciate the value of Deming's principles, as it was not until much later in my career that I recognized that his focus was on developing and implementing an integrated business system in order to achieve superior performance.

Deming preached a philosophy he called *The 14 Principles for Transforming Business Effectiveness.* For more information, read his book, *Out of the Crisis* (MIT Press ed., 2000).

The 14 principles define a system based on integrating the following:

- Leadership
- Product or service quality
- Continuous improvement
- Personal transformation
- Waste minimization
- Building a culture of performance and excellence

His key point was to focus on a system.

We can all learn from Deming and apply a system approach to our own businesses and lives. The trick is to take a step back and to first understand your product or service and the value-added process that makes that product or service a reality. Only then can you discover ways to streamline the process, eliminate duplication, and apply innovation in an integrated manner to effectively deliver a better product at a lower cost.

Are there other areas of your life that can be improved with a system, such as financial planning, wealth management, shopping, career planning, education and managing the home?

Here is how to develop and implement your own system:

Just Start. Don't procrastinate. Start with whatever you have in front of you right now, and improve it as you proceed.

Keep It Simple. By making it easy to implement and manage, you are more likely to maintain it. This leaves you free to focus more on achieving the goals and less on managing the process.

Make It Portable. Whether digital or paper-based, make your system mobile so you can refer to it and update it regularly.

Make It Easy and Cheap to Implement. Avoid very expensive software programs, unnecessary overhead and other infrastructure. Go basic.

Build Your Systems with Scalability in Mind. It may make the initial investment more costly, but the payoff will be worth it in the long run.

Focus on Results, Not Activities. This will ensure you are putting your attention where it counts: on progress, not busywork. Eliminate or outsource low-value activities.

HABIT 70

IF IT IS IMPORTANT, CONTROL IT

"A person who has never made a mistake never tried anything new." | Albert Einstein

When I was a young engineer, I learned a very important lesson about product development and manufacturing. While the design was the interesting aspect of bringing a new product to market, its success or failure was largely due to the systems and structure around it.

Most successful product companies keep a very tight control over the most critical aspects of product design, launch and manufacturing, ensuring not only the success of the product but also the ongoing success of the whole company. If it is important, then nothing is left to chance.

You can apply this same thinking to your own life by treating major projects as a product launch where <u>you</u> control what is important. There is no shame in being meticulous about controlling your own destiny and being focused on all aspects of a project or task that is critical to your success. If it is imperative that it be done right, you must not lose control of the situation.

We often find that critical resources are beyond our control for a variety of reasons, and that we are stymied from achieving the one thing that is most important since we did not make the effort to control it. Access to capital is a good example. If you are serious about your financial future and the freedom that comes along with it, then it is absolutely necessary to have excellent access to capital—either cash, borrowed funds, or assets that can be converted to cash. These opportunities often require capital on relatively short notice, but that can be difficult. However, poor record keeping, poor credit scores, poor relationships with bank managers, contractor liens, and other items can move the access to capital beyond your control. *If it's important, take action and control it thoroughly!*

Now you will immediately be labeled a control freak by people who don't understand your intention, people who are losing because you are winning, or people who are jealous, envious or downright incapable.

To control things well, do the following:

Focus on What is Important. Take total control of it. Control only things that are important, like your health, your financial future and your children's education.

Make the Final Decision. Determine who else is involved in the decision-making or who will impact those decisions, and then ask if they are worthy of your trust. Control does not mean you do everything, but you should, at least, oversee everything important and then monitor even the smallest details. *Don't become complacent.*

Think in Terms of Risk Mitigation. For the business owner, maintaining control is critical to mitigating risk and ensuring your vision is implemented. Think it through and focus on what is most important, and share it with the team around you.

If you are uncomfortable with the term control, then reframe it in your mind as self-reliance. I have never heard anyone called a self-reliance freak! Remind yourself each day why you are becoming self-reliant and that the reward will be worth the effort.

HABIT 71

TAKE ONE ACTION DAILY TOWARD YOUR GOALS

"Only put off until tomorrow what you are willing to die having left undone." | Pablo Picasso

I once walked a section of the Camino de Santiago Pilgrimage, which is a 500-mile ancient pilgrimage route from Southern France to the city of Santiago de Compostela in northwest Spain. Initially, I was daunted by the idea of walking great distances, but soon found out that the task could be accomplished by breaking the trip into manageable pieces. The trip could be broken into days, the days into sections, the sections into hours, and each hour was simply a question of putting one foot in front of the other. I was astonished by how much I could achieve each day by simply putting one foot in front of the other.

Any progression in life is gradual: nature changes slowly through evolution, the mountains fall over time through erosion, the seasons change a little every day. Muscles strengthen or weaken daily. Children grow up daily to become adults. Change is happening around us, and all the time, often imperceptibly, but always happening.

Achieve your own goals by consistently doing one small thing toward their achievement each and every day. By doing even one small action toward your goals, you are forming the habit of achievement, keeping it at the top of your mind, demonstrating a commitment to a worthwhile idea and building a culture of action within your own mindset. There should be no off days or down days toward its achievement.

One action each day, no matter how small, will have a cumulative effect and help you move steadily toward achievement.

Here are some examples of how to put this principle into practice:

If your goal is health and fitness oriented, work on your diet and exercise a little bit every day. Do a daily workout routine and read a blog on wellness.

If your goal is to achieve financial independence, read a chapter of a finance book every day, listen to a podcast, research one investment, make a decision, update your budget or watch your discretionary spending.

If your goal is to be a better parent, take a moment to list three things that can be done to help your child today, or work on your temperament or parenting skills, or organize your home a bit better.

There are many little things you can do each day to achieve your goal. Each action will compound, the steps will turn into miles and, before you know it, you will be well on your way to achieving great things. *A massive and seemingly insurmountable goal can be broken down into smaller steps that will make it easier to accomplish.*

ACTIONS FOR TRACTION

What distractions are causing you to lose focus and how can you eliminate them?

_____

_____

_____

What area of your life needs a *Mastermind,* and who would be in it?

_____

_____

_____

What is your biggest obstacle to getting things done and how can it be eliminated?

_____

_____

_____

What one action can you take today that will massively help you move toward your goals?

_____

_____

_____

CHAPTER 11

STAYING MOTIVATED

"Ask and it will be given to you; seek, and you will find; knock and the door will be opened for you." | Jesus

MY STORY: NEAR DEATH BRINGS MORE LIFE

Staying motivated in order to persevere through great difficulty has been one of my most significant personal challenges. It takes tremendous stamina and mental fortitude to stick with a task and overcome the substantial obstacles that are the inevitable part of progress. Periodically, life helpfully provides a catalyst for motivation through some sort of significant emotional event (like being fired or experiencing an unfortunate loss). These events serve to remind us of the fragility of life while simultaneously providing decades worth of motivational fuel.

One such significant emotional event happened to me when I was 19 years old and almost drowned in a very serious boating accident. I had gone sailing in English Bay, the inner harbor of Vancouver, BC, with my sister, in a small two-person sailboat called a Laser. As often happens on the west coast of Canada, even in the summer months, there can be severe and rapid changes in weather. In our case, the wind picked up shortly after we left shore and in the middle of the harbor, we capsized. It was my fault, as I was captaining the boat and was ultimately responsible for our safety.

My sister fell into the water on the windward side of the boat, meaning that the wind pushed her against the boat. I, on the other hand, fell into the water on the leeward side of the boat, causing the wind to push me away from the boat. On this particular day, the wind was very strong. I started to swim back toward the boat; however, every time I completed a stroke and reached out to grab the side of the boat, I fell short, as I was being pushed slightly further away by the wind. As the wind inevitably pushed me further and further away from the safety of the boat, I remember shouting to my sister, who was clinging on for dear life, "Whatever you do, don't let go of the boat!" Stating the obvious was probably not the best piece of advice I could give her at that time, but it was the overriding thought in my mind.

I was quickly blown away from the boat by the wind, and in a matter of minutes, it was nowhere to be seen. Thankfully, I was being pushed toward the beaches of Vancouver. The Pacific Ocean is quite cold in that area, even in the summer months. Fortunately, I was wearing a lifejacket and knew I only had to wait it out before being gently tossed up onto the beach and the crisis would be over. The strong wind continued to pick up, and I turned my back to the waves so they would wash over my head as I bobbed up and down. I would take a breath between the waves as I bobbed up, and prepared for the next dunking as I bobbed down. I had some difficulty staying motivated, but I also felt sure that the wind would eventually blow me right onto the shore.

However, just when I thought things could not get any worse, I looked toward the harbor and saw a tugboat pulling a massive barge directly toward me. I was terrified and felt a wave of panic sweep over me.

After a few minutes of frantically waving my arms to attract attention, the tugboat captain saw me and came to a complete stop in order to prevent me from being run over. However, the barge behind the tugboat was being moved by the tide and momentum caused it to continue directly toward me. I could immediately see that it was in my direct path. If I could not move out of the way, eventually I'd be swept underneath and I would drown. I did my best to swim away from the path of the barge, but the bulkiness of my clothes, the wind and the tide prevented me from making much progress. The barge seemed to descend upon me very rapidly, and when it was within a few hundred feet I could see a wall of water churning as the waves crashed against the front of it.

At this moment, I knew the situation was very serious and started to lose hope; this was the point of my maximum depression. I was feeling utterly lost. I was only 19 years old, had gone out on a leisurely sailing trip and now, minutes later, I was facing certain death. I felt resentful and cheated. My life was only getting started, and now it was going to be snatched away from me. The situation looked hopeless.

I was starting to give up as the barge moved forward, and now I could hear the roar of the wall of water in front of the barge; I must have been less than a few hundred feet from being swept under. It was at this moment that an extraordinary thing happened: as crazy as it seems, I literally saw an image flash before my eyes. It looked like a large movie screen flashing upon the sky for a few seconds, I do not know if it was a hallucination or what it was, but I saw an image that looked like the front page of the local newspaper. It said 'Man Drowns in English Bay.' First, a jolt of absolute terror went through my entire body as I realized that I might actually die. This was followed by a profound sense of determination. I thought to myself, "I'm too young to die. I am only 19." I had a surge of motivation to get myself out of the situation. I don't know what it was or what triggered it, whether it was hope, despair or my family, but I knew I had to survive. I was motivated!

I looked directly at the barge, which was moving quickly toward me. When it got close, I noticed the cable that connected the tugboat to the barge was cutting through the water like a knife, about 30 feet in front of the barge. It was creating its own wake since it was moving very quickly. I decided that this was my lifeline and lined myself up with the cable. As it came near me, I had one chance to reach out and grab it, which I did. Immediately, I was dragged through the water by the force of the barge, but held on for dear life while hearing the deafening, churning wall of water directly behind me.

I needed to save myself, and I attempted to climb up the cable so I could sit on top of the barge and wait for rescue. But hypothermia was slowly setting in, and I didn't have enough strength to lift myself more than a few feet out of the water. Desperately, I hung onto the cable. After a few minutes, I was spotted by a local boater who courageously approached, threw me a life ring with a rope attached to his boat, and hauled me on board to safety. I was brought by ambulance to the hospital and subsequently released without any problems. My sister, who had also been brought to the same hospital, was treated and released.

This near-death experience gave me a profound sense of the fragility of life and deepened my resolve to make something of myself while I can, since I never know when the situation may change.

The experience taught me to never despair, never give up and always maintain a sense of optimism. It has helped me build the habit of staying motivated during difficult times, and has made it easier to find the strength to persevere and never quit.

HABIT 72

MAXIMIZE ALL RESOURCES AVAILABLE TO YOU

"Success is peace of mind, which is a direct result of self-satisfaction in knowing you did your best to become the best you are capable of becoming." | Coach John Wooden

Rarely do we take the time to truly understand all the resources available to us, and then leverage those resources to make a massive change in our lives. There is timidity in the face of opportunity. Often, we don't understand or appreciate the incredible richness of resources we already have. When we find ourselves in a difficult situation, we tend to go back to the same solution that worked in the past, even if it is not suitable for today.

Our most precious resources are most often free and available in great abundance: time, liberty, love, family bonds, clean air and water, and the freedom to pursue our happiness, prosperity and wealth. Over the course of our lives, we accumulate other important resources, such as education, professional relationships, skills, contacts, reputation, industry knowledge and character traits.

Developing the habit of leveraging these resources starts with a mindset of focusing on what you have, not what you are missing. If your attention is focused on what you lack, no amount of resources will ever be sufficient to help you achieve your goals. However, if your attention is focused on what you have, then you will constantly be reminded of it and attract more into your life.

To maximize your resources:

Make a List of All the Resources Available to You. This includes your network, skills, financial resources, partners and family. Take the time to review the list and determine the best resource for the problem you are currently facing.

Get a New Perspective. Don't only use the same approach that you have used in the past; be creative and try something new.

Maximize Your Network. You do not have to solve your problem by yourself. Reach out to your network and leverage the *Mastermind* concept.

Use Time Effectively. We tend to think we are under time pressure to achieve a certain goal, and sometimes we do have real time constraints. However, it often makes sense to change the timeline or deadline to attack the problem more fully. Most deadlines are artificial; they are there to keep us motivated. However, you may need to work longer hours (a form of resource) in order to maintain a must-hit deadline.

Know Your Skill Set. We often have incredible skills that we do not realize or fully utilize. Take an inventory of your skills, understand what you are missing, and figure out how you might go out and get it. Maybe you need to hire somebody or outsource a particular project.

Speak Often of the Good Things in Your Life. Make a list and read through it regularly, speak about the important resources in your life in a loving and respectful way, and avoid any thought, reference or word about what you are missing, even in jest.

By maximizing all the resources that you have available to you, you can throw everything you have at a problem to help resolve it.

HABIT 73

BUILD STRONG BONDS OF LOVE AND HOPE

"The Scriptures assure me that on the last day we will not be examined on what we believe, but on what we did. Our entrance to heaven will not be because we kneeled and said, "Lord, Lord," but because we did some good for our fellow creatures." | Benjamin Franklin

Staying motivated while doing big and important things is hard work, particularly for a sustained period of time. It can be tough, as you feel that you are literally being worn down and wasting away with fatigue. If the task is difficult but enjoyable and aligned with your values, it becomes an easier burden to bear. If the task is difficult, unenjoyable and not aligned with your values, you may still need to do it, but you may need some help along the way.

That help can come in the form of support, care and consideration from those who care most for you. However, cultivating those relationships does not happen overnight, and they certainly don't take place on short notice because you happen to be in a slump.

If you follow these three simple ideas, you can build solid lifetime relationships and genuine bonds of love:

First, Never Take People for Granted, Especially Family and Close Friends. Take time each day to show a sincere interest in those around you. For a moment, forget that you are not the center of the universe and that other people have hopes, fears and aspirations of their own. Ask them how their day was and then actually listen. Do small favors. Make the extra effort to make them feel important. They will notice it and reciprocate.

Second, Stay Connected. Many years ago, one of the big telephone companies featured a TV commercial meant to encourage greater long-distance calling. Its tagline was 'Reach out and touch someone.' I still think that is great advice today. I know the point of the ad was to sell, but it is a good reminder to call someone not only when you need something, but to actually connect at an emotional level. We can build bonds of love and hope by connecting in a profound way with those we care for. Be authentic, be genuine and use the moment to truly let them know that they are important and that you are there for them. They will be there for you someday.

Finally, Give Without Expectations of Anything in Return. I always put this in the category of easy to say, but hard to do. Human beings have very good BS detectors. So if you call someone after a prolonged absence, he or she will likely suspect you want something. If you only call and ask for something, the relationship is diminished. If you don't, they will be pleasantly surprised, and trust grows. If you call people when you don't need to, and ask what you can do for them, they will be there for you when you need them most.

HABIT 74

SURROUND YOURSELF WITH INSPIRATION

"Live in the sunshine, swim the sea, and drink the wild air." | Ralph Waldo Emerson

One of the best ways to stay motivated during difficult times is to be in an inspirational environment. It is very difficult, if not impossible, to achieve great goals if you are not surrounded by the right people and the right environment. It is critical to create an inspirational habitat. I am referring to an environment where you feel your best. Whether it is inside or outside, in an office or in a home, it must be an environment that inspires you to be your best and achieve great things.

How can you create an inspiring workspace?

Know Where You Do Your Best Work. Examine what aspects of that environment have the greatest effect on you and replicate them in a separate workspace dedicated to your best work.

Have Space that You Fully Control. Make this your own space. This is a place where you are going to achieve great things. Don't let anyone else interfere with it.

Be Aware of the Impact of Your Surroundings. Set an environment that has a positive impact on you. This requires being introspective about what makes and keeps you motivated.

Improve Your Environment Over Time. As your circumstances change, update your office, your work environment and your home accordingly. Don't let it become stale. Work with it over time to make it the best it can be.

HABIT 75

DETERMINE THE CAUSES OF STRESS AND ELIMINATE THEM

*"Everything you've ever wanted is on
the other side of fear."* | George Addair

Stress can be a terrible thing, especially chronic stress over a sustained period. A little bit of stress may be worthwhile, but a large amount will take its toll on you. Anything you can do to eradicate or reduce excessive stress will help you achieve more. Sometimes the source of your stress is hard to pinpoint. I personally have often gone through periods of great stress without really understanding why.

Although it may sound counterintuitive, I have found it very helpful to sit down periodically and make a list of all the things in my life that are causing me stress.

When I make my list, although some of the stressors turn out to be the cumulative effects of several stressful things in my life, many times they are the result of only a few factors. After completing my list, I go through it and determine ways to reduce each stressor. The process of making the list in itself is helpful. Having a plan in place to reduce the effects of each stressor gives me greater peace of mind.

Once you've finished making a list, begin executing your plans. Usually, the execution involves removing certain things, as we often get stressed when we are trying to do too much. We become less effective when we lack focus. Reducing or eliminating the distractions of some activities or certain people will improve your situation by helping you focus. You will find that you can reduce many stressors and even eliminate some completely.

Take a moment to begin writing down your list of stressors and brainstorm ways to mitigate them. Repeat this process over the course of several days, and you will find that your focus will move from the causes of stress to the actions needed to eliminate stress.

HABIT 76

CULTIVATE AN ATTITUDE OF GRATITUDE

"The only person you are destined to become is the person you decide to be." | Ralph Waldo Emerson

It may be difficult to be gracious when you find yourself in a negative mental state, but developing an attitude of gratitude is critical to long-term success. It gives you a sense of ease and calm, which is important to living a good life. It makes you more grounded, more pleasant to work with and more enjoyable to be around.

There are three things that I do to maintain an attitude of gratitude:

I focus on being thankful for the small positive things that happen throughout the day. This focuses my mind on what I have, rather than what I lack. Finished a good workout—thank you! Enjoyed some time with the family—thank you! Signed up a new customer—thank you!

I keep a short list of things for which I am thankful. I read through that list every now and then. It's a great reminder of my gratitude for my family, health, city and country, for instance. By reading through that list, I start to feel better and more grateful for the things that I have.

I pray to a higher power. I have deep faith and belief that God will continue to bring abundance into my life. So I pray to God on a daily basis, being thankful for abundance in my life now and for the abundance yet to come.

GET AN ACCOUNTABILITY PARTNER TO KEEP YOU ON TRACK

"People often say that motivation doesn't last. Well, neither does bathing. That's why we recommend it daily." | Zig Ziglar

We all need to be held accountable. Nobody is completely self-sufficient to the point that they do not need anyone to help keep them on track. Even the world's most successful entrepreneurs have built a team of people who hold them accountable, maybe not directly, but as a working partnership.

Accountability partnerships are the basis for an entire industry of fitness trainers, coaches and weight loss practitioners, among others. Business partnerships succeed largely due to the accountability of partners. In good marriages, there is a balance between support and accountability, which helps to build long-term marital happiness and a strong family.

Accountability partners help us overcome the human nature tendency to take the path of least resistance. They build discipline into our lives and ensure we have people around us who will have the insight to know our weaknesses, the courage to confront us with making a change, and the perseverance to stick with us as we progress. It's not a boss; instead, it's a partner, with a shared vision and destiny, who will care and want to see us succeed.

Here's a great way to get started with an accountability partner:

Find the Right Partner. Pick someone who is trustworthy, an expert in his or her field, and whose interests are completely in line with your own.

Decide on a Big Goal. Pick the one big goal in your life that you want to improve, and know precisely why you want to improve it.

Pick a Method of Accountability. You may find that a regularly scheduled meeting (like a weekly conference call) will work well, or that appropriate incentives will keep you motivated.

Be Open to Honest Feedback By Seeking the Truth. It is critical to work with someone who is knowledgeable and trustworthy, so the feedback is coming from a place of expertise and love. Listen respectfully to your accountability partner's advice and take it when it makes sense.

HABIT 78

FORGET WORK-LIFE BALANCE, SEEK WORK-LIFE HARMONY

"The key is not to prioritize what's on your schedule, but to schedule your priorities." | Stephen Covey

Work-life balance is a phrase that easily rolls off the tongue in a way that tends to appeal to everyone. However, I don't think many people really think it through, as it has different meanings to different people. I have always had a philosophical problem with the concept of work-life balance, since the concept of balance, in its very nature, refers to opposing forces canceling each other out to maintain equilibrium.

People who refer to work-life balance are generally considering their work in opposition to their life, and therefore see the need for balance. If they loved what they were doing, there would be harmony, not disharmony, and they would be referring to work-life harmony.

I understand that we all need to work for a variety of reasons: to provide for ourselves and our families, to contribute to the community in a meaningful way, or to fulfill our human potential. But work need not be in opposition to life: it should complement life.

It is unreasonable to think that you can have a balance between work and living (non-work activities) through all phases of your life. The reality is that our professional and personal demands vary wildly over the course of our lifetime.

I think a better way to manage work-life harmony is to clarify your priorities over the long term and then use good time management skills to handle each day. For example, young parents may decide to devote more time to their family when the children are younger; therefore, the scale swings toward the life side, only to swing toward more work later in life when the children are older. A short-term business or promotional opportunity may cause a busy executive to dedicate themselves to work more for a shorter period of time, only to ease off at a later date.

Understand your circumstances and make priority adjustments over a long-term horizon while maintaining excellent short-term time management skills. At the same time, strive to find more harmony in making your work your life, so that you are doing something you enjoy and it does not feel like work.

Be very careful when you say work-life balance; focus on finding work-life harmony instead!

ACTIONS FOR TRACTION

Make a comprehensive list of all the resources available to you.

_____

_____

_____

Describe what an inspiring workplace would look like for you and how you can make it happen.

_____

_____

_____

Who or what is causing you great stress, and how can it be reduced?

_____

_____

_____

What are you thankful for today?

_____

_____

_____

CHAPTER 12

ACHIEVING FINANCIAL SUCCESS

"Money isn't the most important thing in life, but it's reasonably close on the 'gotta have it' scale." | Zig Ziglar

MY STORY: THE FIRST RUNG ON THE PROPERTY LADDER

Zig Ziglar was right: money may not be the most important thing in the world, but it is certainly near the top of the list! Even if you don't think money is important at all, you still need some to buy food, pay rent, get around, and periodically go to the doctor or dentist. Try doing any of those without money!

I have always made the direct connection between money and freedom. I have never seen a free broke person. *To me, it's not money that counts, it's what I can DO with money that counts.* This important distinction is often lost on people, or simply ignored by the money-doesn't-buy-you-happiness crowd. Technically, they are right, since happiness is not a commodity like grain or coal that can be bought. However, practically, money can buy the things and circumstances that create happiness and freedom. Freedom from worry, poor health, disease, lack, ignorance and other obstacles to happiness. I can speak from personal experience, since I have had periods of my life with money and without it, and I clearly know which I prefer.

As my career progressed from getting a formal education to becoming a corporate executive and finally to launching my own business, my views on money have changed. I have now come to believe that each of us has a financial or money blueprint, often set at a young age, that significantly shapes our financial mindset. The mindset can be reinforced by those around us and by our own actions, and it can either be very positive or very negative, or somewhere in between. It is important to be aware of your own financial blueprint and respond accordingly.

In my particular case, my mother was risk averse, focused on job security and frugality to the point where I literally received Canada Savings Bonds certificates on my birthday. I understand and appreciate that she did this out of love and concern for her children and our financial futures. My father, on the other hand, was entrepreneurial, and would buy and sell almost anything. Throughout my childhood, I saw him trade cars and trucks (many), boats, furniture, antiques, clothing (including 3,000 pairs of overalls) and even anti-vandal paint that never dried (for which he charged a premium!). Even though he did not have formal training, he had a natural instinct for making money. Truly, financial success is about what you make, keep, invest and then grow. I ended up somewhere in between my parents: a relatively conservative investor, willing to take the risk for the right opportunity, sometimes too frugal and security-minded, but always focused on capital preservation.

My father was very interested in real estate and at one point he owned multiple real estate properties in Vancouver, which was quite an accomplishment, considering that his full-time trade was a millwright. As soon as I started earning income, the idea of owning real estate greatly appealed to me. This idea was compounded vividly at the end of each month when I paid my rent to a landlord and knew I would never see that money again.

My own particular story about real estate is about getting on the property ladder. Starting in my late 20s, after having only been working for four or five years, my wife and I decided that we wanted to buy our own house. We did whatever it took to get our money together; we were 100% committed and did not hesitate. Even though we were living in Toronto, we intended to buy a house in Vancouver. We were 100% committed and did not hesitate. We maximized our earnings at the time and we minimized our expenses by literally living on fumes, including both of us living in a 350-square-foot studio apartment in order to save rent. Minimal holidays for many years (but lots of camping trips), one car, daily brown bag lunches, and working seven days a week to earn extra overtime and bonus money.

The idea was to put everything we had toward our first home, knowing that once we bought it, we would immediately start building equity. We scraped together a down payment of about $50,000 (in 1990 dollars) through a combination of credit cards, lines of credit, and some cash, and by collapsing investment accounts. We bought our first house, paying a 13% mortgage rate. Over time, we added considerable sweat equity, paid down the debt and upgraded houses. We were always trying to find something we could add value to, so we were not necessarily paying top dollar. We gained knowledge each year as we continued to enjoy not only living in the home but also the benefits of compounding equity.

While we have had ups and downs, like any family, our respect for earning and keeping money has never diminished. Sometimes we become too complacent, especially when things are going very well. We took some risks early in our careers, which paid off largely due to the effect of compounding and maintaining a relatively frugal lifestyle. To this day, the two of us still meet and review our financial status weekly, ensuring we understand how to maintain and grow what we have accumulated so far, and keeping current on changes in the economy and our own financial picture. We never take what we have accumulated for granted, and we are thankful for the blessings we have received.

The definition of financial success is different for each person, but the process of achieving it is common. It starts with a burning desire to be financially independent by creating value for others, and being rewarded correspondingly. Finally, it is about securing what you have worked hard to achieve, giving where you can, but never becoming complacent as you continue along the road to building wealth.

KNOW YOUR RELATIONSHIP WITH MONEY AND ITS ROOT CAUSE

"If you look at what you have in life, you'll always have more. If you look at what you don't have in life, you'll never have enough." | Oprah Winfrey

Most of us have an emotional relationship with money. This relationship is often established at a young age, primarily under the influence of our family, environment and circumstances at the time. It can be positive or negative. However, not all of us realize how it affects our day-to-day decision-making and long-term accumulation of wealth.

For instance, if you associate money largely with consumption and raising your social status, then as you accumulate wealth later on in life, you may focus on enhancing your social status, at the risk to capital preservation. If you see money as a source for good in your community when you are young, you may be attracted to it and use it to improve your own life and the lives of many other people. If you resent wealthy people or are jealous of others who have accumulated wealth, these feelings will foster a negative relationship with money, and you may find it difficult to attract money in sufficient quantities.

You can determine your relationship with money by critically observing your own behaviors regarding investing, spending, personal finances and wealth management. Do you treat money with respect by budgeting well, being frugal and maintaining good account balances? If so, you likely have a positive relationship with money. Are you frivolous with your money? Do you find bills crumpled in your pocket, not know precisely how your investments are doing or feel jealous of the financial success of your friends or family? Then your relationship may be more negative.

Observe your own language and emotion around money. When referring to money do you use terms like 'filthy rich,' 'sick' or 'dirty,' or more positive terms like 'manage' or 'take care of'? When you see someone in a very expensive car, do you assume that the driver worked hard for his or her money, or do you attribute it to the proceeds of crime? Do you say that 'money is the root of all evil'? The actual Bible quote reads "For the <u>love</u> of money is a root of all kinds of evils. It is through this craving that some have wandered away from the faith and pierced themselves with many pangs." (Timothy 6:10).

Understand your relationship with money and what money can do for you, your family and your community. It can be a source of great liberty. It can also give you financial and social stability, and quality education for your children and for multiple generations to come. It can build hospitals, schools, churches, synagogues and mosques for your community.

Take some time to consider your relationship with money: how you handle it and how you view it. Speak to those who are closest to you—your spouse, business partner or close friend—to see if they can offer any insight into your relationship with money.

If you find you need to take corrective action, do so immediately. Build relationships with people with the right money mindset, immerse yourself in a positive relationship with money, and expunge all people from your life who reinforce any negative stereotypes you may have. Start immediately to associate positive benefits with having money, and treat the accumulation of wealth as a critical step in helping yourself, so you can help your family in a profound way.

HABIT 80

GET A PROPER FINANCIAL EDUCATION

*"An investment in knowledge pays
the best interest."* | Benjamin Franklin

Our economy is financially complex. Therefore, a rudimentary understanding of finances and economics is critical for success, to both survive and thrive in this changing world.

Unfortunately, our educational system fails to properly educate young people with a fundamental financial education. Young people may turn to their parents for assistance, but many parents' understanding of financial matters is inadequate to assist themselves, never mind their children. They often pass off their bad habits to their children, thinking that they are helping them when they are actually hurting them.

This can have a significant, material and catastrophic impact. A proper financial education for you and your family is paramount, especially if you aspire to the accumulation of multigenerational wealth.

Your financial matters are your own responsibility. The foundation of financial success starts with a solid financial education, which does not necessarily need to be advanced degrees or complex programs. First, accumulate the basic financial knowledge required to survive in society, and then accumulate more advanced financial knowledge, perhaps for your profession, family business or personal interests.

To accumulate this financial knowledge, do the following:

Recognize and Remind Yourself that the Accumulation of Wealth is Your Personal Responsibility. The government will not help you. Even if you come from a wealthy family and expect to receive an inheritance, circumstances for any family can change. Acceptance of your responsibility is the first step in a proper financial education.

Complete a Realistic Assessment of Your Financial Knowledge. Consult online resources, books or your professional circle. Use these tools to find out exactly what information you are missing. Do not sugarcoat it; be honest with yourself. Your future and your family's future are at stake.

Be Systematic in Acquiring Basic Financial Knowledge. Maintain structure and discipline, such as taking night school courses, an online program or some other similar program in order to acquire the knowledge you need.

Surround Yourself with People Who Have More Advanced Financial Knowledge Than You Do. If your parents are not wealthy, do not ask them how to generate significant amounts of money or wealth. You might feel comfortable talking to them, and they may think they know what they are doing, but they may not. Instead, join an established group, with the right knowledge. If there are none available, create your own.

Provide Your Children with the Financial Education They Need to Be Successful. They are not getting the knowledge they need in the school system. Buy them good books and magazines, and talk to them about the importance of financial education. Instead of giving them things, have them earn an allowance and then use it to pay for consumer items they wish to purchase. Discuss both the successes and failures you are having as a family. Give them the gift not of consumption but of production, so rather than having a consumer mindset, they will have a producer mindset. They will be frugal wealth-builders, ensuring their success and the success of their children for many years to come.

HABIT 81

THINK ONLY ABUNDANCE, NOT LACK

"You become what you believe." | Oprah Winfrey

From when we wake up in the morning until we go to bed, every moment of our day is filled with thoughts. Like a long freight train crossing the Prairies, our thoughts are a seemingly endless stream of consciousness, filling us with emotion, and forming the basis of the actions we take throughout the day.

In this age of information, we are surrounded by thousands of daily reminders of lack. Most of this comes from advertising, as it causes you to feel fear and lack by promoting what you don't have, in order to sell more. Your association with certain friends, colleagues and family members may also cause you to feel lack, as they may also experience lack in their lives.

The message we often hear throughout the day is about what we are missing, not what we have. Think about how many times you have heard something along the lines of *"Congratulations! You have everything you need right now, and the most important things are free! Health, fresh air, family and liberty! Don't buy a thing."*

Whether financially or in other ways, it is imperative to focus on abundance and to avoid any thoughts of lack.

Try the following:

Dissociate Yourself from People Who Chronically Think in Terms of Lack. This is particularly important if they have the annoying habit of wanting to share their lack thinking with you. Whether they're friends or family, let them go.

Severely Limit Your Exposure to Media. Traditional forms of media tend to emphasize consumption and lack, and de-emphasize productivity and abundance.

Admire Other Successful and Rich People. I keep about 12 photographs in my study of people I admire (e.g., Terry Fox, Ernest Shackleton, Oprah Winfrey) that help inspire me when the going gets tough.

Stay Busy. Dramatically ramp up action or take some bold initiative, to the point of being too busy to think about what you do not have.

Focus on Two or Three Things that Keep You Motivated Each Day. This may be in the form of an inspirational quote, some photos, a book you admire or a friend who helps you. Find a few things you can do every day to help direct your mind toward the abundance that exists in this world and how to bring more of it into your own life.

ALWAYS BE OPPORTUNITY-ORIENTED

"Business opportunities are like buses, there is always another one coming." | Richard Branson

Seeing growth opportunities requires instinct and courage. It's the combination of taking frequent, small, structured steps daily while seizing infrequent, large, unstructured opportunities when they present themselves. These large opportunities are usually the events in our lives that, from a financial perspective, transform us and our families. The daily rigorous and structured steps we take prepare us for these opportunities. Using a sports analogy, think of the small steps as **defense** and the big opportunities as **offense**.

When these opportunities appear, it requires boldness and courage to seize them by becoming mentally prepared to take action. These big opportunities occur infrequently, perhaps only once or twice a year. *However, with good judgment, when you see it and it looks good, pounce on it! Do not procrastinate or be fearful; be courageous.*

Keep opportunity in the forefront of your mind. For example, have you ever had the experience of buying a new car, and on the way home it looks like every second car on the road is the same as the one you just bought? Our brain has tuned into that particular car, so that's what we see. Opportunities are like that, but the brain must be trained and in tune.

Here are the six things you can do to become more opportunity-oriented:

1. Recognize that virtually every significant opportunity you will encounter will be created from an idea or a hunch. Nobody will deliver you a blue ribbon opportunity, so don't wait for the phone to ring or for someone to knock on the door; go find it yourself.

2. Most of the best opportunities come from specialized knowledge circumstances, so you need to become a specialized insider. It will be rare that, as an outsider or a generalist, you will find an opportunity that no one else has seen. It will likely come from an association with your business, practice, hobby, family or some activity in which you are involved. So stay super busy, get involved in serious projects and always be on the lookout.

3. Look at the world differently. Be curious, probe and try to understand what is causing problems in the world, and how you can fix them. If you see something that seems out of the ordinary, dig a little further and see if an opportunity exists. Ignore the naysayers.

4. Treat problems that come along as potential opportunities. I have seen many circumstances where some of the best financial deals are wrapped in the cloak of a problem. For instance, a poor tenant situation or a run-down home in a good area could lead to a good real estate deal; a broken business with phenomenal technical expertise and customer list could be a turnaround candidate. Embrace the problems.

5. Finally, take massive action, dig deep and never take your foot off the accelerator. If you suspect that an opportunity may be there, do not procrastinate, do not even wait one day or one minute: pursue it immediately and aggressively.

6. Preserve and build the opportunity muscle. Even though many leads will be dead ends, get into the habit of pursuing leads. You will often find that you can dig something else up in the process.

Being opportunity-oriented is a life-changing mindset. If you seize these rare and special events, you can transform your life in a non-linear way, and accumulate wealth and happiness much more quickly.

HABIT 83

GO THE EXTRA MILE

"There are no traffic jams along the
extra mile." | Roger Staubach

Some of us fall into the habit of expecting to be paid first and then create value later, under the false thinking that we will only create value once we have been compensated. The reality is different. In the marketplace called life, I believe in the motto of *Where The Value Goes, Money Grows.* Getting into the habit of creating value first is a lifelong mindset change that affects the accumulation of wealth and the understanding of money.

There is a direct connection between value creation and compensation. The bigger the problem you solve, the greater the value you create for other people, the more they reciprocate and the greater your compensation. If you want to become a billionaire, help a billion people. The people who go above and beyond what is required are the ones who will stick out from the crowd and be rewarded accordingly, having put forth their best effort for the compensation.

So, how do you get into the habit of creating value first?

Be Service-Oriented. Treat every interaction, particularly in a business environment, as a chance to serve others. Even if you are not directly involved in a transaction at the time, find a way to be of some service to the person you are dealing with, without the expectation of compensation every single time. It will come with time.

Understand the Difference Between Good Enough and Excellent. Good enough is average; excellence is world-class. Pursue excellence in everything you do, and you will find that you need to go above and beyond in all aspects of your life, which will make you better, more noticed and more valuable.

Learn to Postpone Financial Gratification. Becoming wealthy takes time, so you need a pool of capital, and time, to generate yield. Get used to it, since there is no get-rich-quick scheme. By postponing gratification, you will get into the habit of making the investment first and seeking the return later.

Use the Extra Mile to Improve Your Personal Brand and Reputation. You are not only fulfilling your brand, but you are building it and moving it to a higher level.

Be Fearless about Sticking Out from the Crowd. Most people will ridicule you for being a suck-up, or too good for them, for consistently going the extra mile. Don't be afraid. This will build grit and perseverance over time, and make you the winner in the long run.

HABIT 84

IGNORE MOST POPULAR PRESS REPORTS ABOUT MONEY

"Education costs money. But then so does ignorance." | *Sir Claus Moser*

According to a recent survey, half of Canadians are within $200 of not being able to pay their bills. Many people in our society today are living paycheck to paycheck, barely making ends meet, and are not successful financially.

They may be comfortable, and might even feel secure, but they are certainly not wealthy, nor are they able to withstand even a minor economic shock to their personal situation. They have been unable to lift themselves up from their circumstances, in part because they listened to people who did not have their vested interest at heart. They are not giving themselves a proper financial education and are associating themselves with the wrong people. When they do seek financial information, they turn to the wrong sources. Rather than speaking with people who are significantly more financially successful than they are, they turn to the popular press for financial information. I believe this is a mistake.

The focus in the popular press is to sell advertising, which is done by making you feel you have a problem. The greater the problem, the more fearful you become, the more you consume and the more you read. *Being sold and fearful will not make you rich.* Keep that in mind with all information from the popular press and mass media in general. *There are a few minor exceptions, but generally avoid what you read in the popular press about money.*

The popular press rarely has the time and financial resources to cover a financial topic comprehensively. I am referring primarily to mass and popular media, not to niche publications that are dedicated to finance, business and wealth creation.

Take the following steps to get quality financial information:

Consult Rich People Who Are at Least 10X Wealthier Than You. Ask them for some help and be prepared to offer something in return. Hide your shame, since they were likely in your circumstance at one point, and simply ask.

Invest in a Superior Financial Education. Follow top-rated financial bloggers; attend great, independent financial conferences; subscribe to world-class financial publications (like *Forbes*); and join groups in your community focused on helping you become rich.

Practice By Doing. You can only learn so much by reading or listening to others. Start small, but start, and you will be amazed how much you learn when there is real money at stake, particularly when it's your own!

HABIT 85

THINK LIKE AN INVESTOR

"I will tell you how to get rich. Close the doors. Be
fearful when others are greedy. Be greedy when
others are fearful." | Warren Buffett

There are a number of obstacles that prevent the average person from building financial wealth. The biggest is having the wrong mindset. You cannot be rich if you don't think rich. The biggest obstacle to achieving financial freedom and success is not what you learned in school (lack of skills, capital or opportunity); it is usually one thing, the wrong mindset.

A mindset is an established way of thinking held by a person or group of people. People tend to act in a way that's consistent with their mindset, past actions and decisions, and it's very difficult to convince them to act otherwise. Consequently, it's challenging to break out of your own mindset, even when you know that it's holding you back from success.

To develop the habit of thinking like an investor or business owner, you must first understand how investors think. Then follow their examples and reinforce them with good habits.

So, what is an investor mindset?

Investors think in terms of asset accumulation and positive cash flow, not liabilities and negative cash flow. An asset is any financial instrument that produces a return and holds its value. It gives your money back.

Investors Are Frugal, Not Cheap. Frugal is the good economic use of scarce resources. Cheap is just spending as little money as possible. Frugal is not wasting what you have, but spending when necessary. Cheap is being fearful of loss, and hoarding what little already exists.

Investors View Opportunity Differently. They are tuned into opportunities, and often see a problem as a way to make money, not lose it. For instance, a run-down looking house may be an eyesore to most, but an investor may see it as an opportunity to buy at a discount and create value.

Investors Acquire Assets and Avoid Most Liabilities. Unless the liabilities help you acquire the assets in a productive way, they are to be avoided. For instance, it makes sense to borrow interest-deductible debt (liability) to purchase a multi-family property (asset) that has good long-term cash flow and potential appreciation.

Investors Associate with Other Investors, Not Consumers. This can be done by joining an investor group, a *Mastermind* or another group you create. The thinking will rub off on you and help you develop better financial habits on your own journey.

Investors View Cash as High Risk and the Accumulation of Assets as Low Risk. Seeking safety means stagnation; investors are constantly looking to move forward.

If you're early in your journey of wealth accumulation, consider buying a modest amount of assets, such as a stock or a bond, in order to understand how assets work. *Nothing clarifies the thinking and sharpens the mind faster than writing a check.* Start small at the beginning until you become more comfortable and knowledgeable, but definitely start.

HABIT 86

FOCUS ON VALUE, NOT COST

"The stock market is filled with individuals
who know the price of everything, but the
value of nothing." | Philip Fisher

Developing the habit of buying the best you can afford will ensure that your money goes further since it is better economics in the long run.

How many times have you tried to save money by buying something slightly cheaper, taking a shortcut, buying secondhand or buying something that was 'good enough'? In the end, did you really save? *We are often penny-wise and pound-foolish, thinking that saving a few pennies by compromising on a product or service will really make a big difference.* The reality is that we end up paying one way or the other. There is really no such thing as cheap! We may not always pay financially, but we do end up paying one way or another.

Milton Friedman was right when he said, "There is no such thing as a free lunch." If we do not pay financially, we may pay with time, frustration or reputation, or in many other ways. But we do pay when we compromise by not getting the best we can afford, particularly if it's for our work or investments. There have been a number of times that I have purchased a slightly inferior product, like clothing, only to find that it wears out twice as fast, does not hold its shape, or looks shabby when I want to feel great. How often have you saved money on a family vacation or got a deal on travel costs, only to find you arrive at a second-rate hotel that's dirty, with poor service, making your holiday something to forget, not remember? It is not worth it!

I am all for frugality and do not feel one should spend a penny more than necessary to achieve good quality; however, I believe that one should buy the best one can afford. There are a few notable cases where frugality can make a big difference. For instance, buying an average quality house in a top neighborhood where you can add value is better than buying a top quality house in an average neighborhood, where there is a devaluation risk. Some very high-end items, such as cars and boats, can be purchased one or two years old, in near-new condition for a deep discount due to rapid depreciation. Some artwork, jewelry or collectibles can be purchased at distressed prices at auction or estate sales, and produce an immediate value creation.

The better approach is to buy the best you can afford. In actual fact, it is often better to buy the best or to buy nothing at all!

When you're considering a large expenditure:

First, Ask Yourself if the Purchase Is Necessary. Often we make purchases based on emotional decisions defined by our financial blueprint and old habits. Take a moment to ask yourself if you really need to make the purchase at all, what is motivating the decision, and if it can be avoided completely or if a better alternative exists. Seriously think it through, or use the decision-making tool I mentioned previously.

Second, Consider Buying Fewer but Better Things. For instance, perhaps a seven-day vacation at a top hotel on the beach is better than a 10-day vacation one block from the water. By staying at the top hotel, you will likely be more relaxed, better served and feel more satisfied (which is the point of a vacation) for no additional total cost. Buying fewer but better quality clothing items, such as suits and jackets, will ensure you look great all the time, and they will likely last twice as long as cheaper alternatives.

Finally, Invest in Quality Infrastructure. In the home office, good quality infrastructure is often much more expensive initially but pays off in the long run. Cheap computers and technology have an uncanny way of failing you at the most critical moment. Cheap construction materials or methods will cost you much more money in the long run, and lose their aesthetic and functional appeal.

HABIT 87

BUY ASSETS AND CREATE PASSIVE INCOME STREAMS

"A wise man should have money in his head,
but not in his heart." | Jonathan Swift

We live in an increasingly complex, expensive world. According to the US Census Bureau and Pew Research, since 1970, the US middle class has shrunk from 53% of the population to about 45%, and the median incomes levels have remained stagnant.

As we age, our ability to support our lifestyle through work diminishes for a variety of reasons, mostly health related. Therefore, it is absolutely critical to accumulate assets that can replace our work as the primary source of our income. This means embarking on a lifelong journey of the accumulation of assets that create passive income streams, until you come to a point in your life where you have the option to continue to work in a traditional sense, without financial risk. If you are in the unfortunate circumstance of having an illness or being unable to work, then passive income streams will enable you to maintain a good quality of life.

Examples of passive income streams include:

- Dividends from a stock portfolio

- Interest from bonds and savings accounts

- Pension income

- Rental income from rental property

- Dividend income from businesses

- Royalties from artistic or intellectual property

- Any other source that provides income on an ongoing basis without significant intervention

If you are in the early part of your career, you still have sufficient time to develop passive income streams. While it may seem difficult with all your other financial obligations, such as day-to-day expenses, education or shelter, the accumulation of assets should be a high priority, even if you're only able to set a small amount aside.

Here are the top ways that I suggest you get into the habit of buying assets and accumulating passive income streams:

Expand Your Means By Aggressively Expanding Your Income. Make the massive expansion of your income a high priority, even if you are in a professional occupation such as law, accounting or medicine. High salaries can be eroded dramatically through taxes, high consumption, and inflation. Take a second job, upgrade your skills to earn more money, move to a better opportunity, or start a business on the side and expand it. There are a lot of different ways to expand your income.

Make It a Priority to Live Within Your Means. Get into the habit of living a frugal life so you have some money left over to invest. This means avoiding a high consumption lifestyle and postponing gratification until you've embarked on a plan of living within your means.

Invest, Do Not Save. Today's low interest rates will likely continue for many years. The income from savings is insufficient to give you enough time to accumulate significant assets, particularly after the inflationary effect is taken into consideration. Focus on investing in assets, not only savings, even if it is a simple portfolio of high-quality, dividend-producing stocks.

If You Are an Employee, Seek All Possible Benefits. If your employer is offering any sort of retirement plan and you are early in your career, seize the opportunity and sign up immediately. You'll need to understand the details of the plan, but chances are that you may be in that role longer than you think. Even a modest plan accumulated over a brief period of time can provide good income later on in life.

Make Real Estate a Priority in Your Asset Accumulation Strategy. We all need a place to live, and if you buy your own principal residence, it can appreciate significantly in value over the course of your life. However, do not overdo it, given the high costs of real estate (both initial and operating costs). If possible, be creative. For example, buying a triplex, living in one suite and renting out the other two will largely cover your costs. Later on in life, that will reverse and turn into a passive income stream.

Turn Your Hobby Into Money. Look for other ways to generate passive income streams in your jobs, hobbies or skills. This is a particularly good way to generate more money, since it can be done outside of your normal work hours (evenings and weekends), and it will be enjoyable. If you like cooking, start a cooking school on Saturday. If food is your thing, build an online community and start selling related products. If rock climbing is your gig, then start a travel blog and turn it into paid tours.

There is virtually no limit to the ways additional income streams can be created. Most people fail, as they run into obstacles and then give up. The key is to focus on one area, and then persevere until the stream is up and running, and then start the next one.

HABIT 88

BECOME WEALTHY FROM THE POWER OF COMPOUNDING

"Success will come when you choose to feed your dreams and starve your doubts." | Robert G. Allen

Have you heard of *The Tale of the Wheat and Chessboard*? It is based on a story about the invention of the game of chess. The story goes that the inventor showed the chessboard to his king, who was so impressed that he asked the inventor to name his own reward for the accomplishment. The inventor, who understood the power of compounding, only asked that he be given a single grain of wheat for the first square, double on the second square and so on for the balance of the board, and the king quickly agreed. The king sent his treasurer away to get the grain for the inventor, but after the treasurer had been gone for a week, the king became worried. He called for the treasurer to ask what had happened and was told that, through the power of compounding, the king owed the inventor 18,446,744,073,709,551,615 grains of wheat! The king had gotten a quick lesson in finance and the power of compounding.

The exponential effect of compounding is quite extraordinary, as the above example illustrates. You don't have to have a math degree to see how the effects of compounding can work to your advantage, particularly if you are early in your life and you maintain a disciplined, structured approach to monthly investment.

For instance, according to a recent CNBC article, a 25-year-old who makes $40,000 per year and contributes 10% of her salary to an investment plan annually will amass $3.9 million by the time she retires at age 67. That figure assumes a 50% employer contribution match, a 5% estimated salary increase rate annually and an 8% rate of return. Using all the same parameters, that same person would have $2.5 million, or $1.4 million less, if she had started saving only five years later at age 30. Due to the power of compounding, a five-year head start results in a significant difference in the total.

When we were children, on the first snowfall we would rush outside to build a snowman. Starting with a handful of snow, we would start rolling the small snowball in the snow until it got so large we could barely push it. Compounding is similar, as the effort is great at the start, but the reward is in the perseverance over time.

My wife and I put three children through university by starting a college fund the month they were born, and contributing only $100 per month into a blue-chip, dividend-producing stock portfolio. The accumulated effect of the monthly contribution, stock price increases and reinvested dividends paid for three college tuitions 18 years later.

Here's how to set yourself up to take advantage of the power of compounding:

Start Early. Start investing as soon as you have even a modest income, preferably in your teenage or early adult years. If you are a parent, encourage good investing habits in your children by setting up an investment account (such as an In-Trust Account) or buying shares in a quality company that produce consistent dividends.

Follow the 10% Rule. Once you start a working career, start immediately investing 10% of your net earnings into solid, blue-chip, dividend-producing stocks. Make sure you select to reinvest the dividends. Live off the balance and never, ever touch the principal.

Be Patient. Hang in for the long haul, since the stock markets will go through long-term trends and short-term periods of intense volatility. This is normal. Resist the temptation to liquidate during a period of significant market meltdown, such as in 2008. Think long-term: decades, not years.

Avoid Mutual Funds. Avoid investments with high fees (above 1%). While the fee may seem small initially, it will eat significantly into your return and be expensive over the long run. Investigate good quality index funds or an Exchange Traded Fund (ETF) as an alternative, or build your own portfolio.

Albert Einstein famously stated "Compounding interest is the eighth wonder of the world. He who understands it earns it. He who doesn't pays it."

If it's good enough for Einstein, it should be good enough for you.

HABIT 89

FOCUS ON WHAT YOU KEEP, NOT ONLY WHAT YOU EARN

"It's not how much money you make, but how much you keep, how hard it works for you, and how many generations you keep it for." | Robert Kiyosaki

The point of building good financial habits is to accumulate the wealth necessary to achieve more important goals, such a helping your family, fulfilling your potential, helping society or creating a legacy. The accumulation of money for the sake of wealth is rare, as most wealthy people are driven by a higher purpose.

It is important to have both an offensive and a defensive strategy: wealth accumulation and wealth preservation strategies. *You need to accumulate as much as you can through skills development, value creation and hard work, and then preserve it through frugal living and sound investment. This combination will enable you to become a prolific accumulator of wealth.*

Unfortunately, many people expand their lifestyles in direct proportion to the expansion of their income, leaving little or no money for capital accumulation. This is particularly a problem for many high-paid professionals like doctors, accountants and lawyers, who feel they need to exhibit high social status for career purposes. They earn high incomes over the course of their professional lives; however, they often do not maintain frugal habits in order to convert that high income into the accumulation of wealth. As they get older and their income starts to drop, they are unable to maintain the lifestyles they have grown accustomed to, and they have not put aside sufficient money for the future.

The focus needs to be on what you keep each month, not on what you make.

To keep more money, do the following:

Pay Yourself First. Each and every month, make sure you are paid first before the bank, government or anyone else in line for your paycheck. Each month, put a fixed amount of your earnings (such as 10%) into an investment account. Live off the balance.

Don't Scale Up Your Lifestyle as Income Rises. As we get older and our income goes up, and there is a tendency to start switching to a consumption lifestyle: bigger house, bigger car, big screen TV. In the end, the difference between what we make and what we keep does not change, or in many cases, it gets worse, even though our income is higher. Avoid the temptation and learn to live with what you have. Don't try to keep up with the Joneses.

Use Debt for Investment, Not Consumption. Avoid most forms of debt for consumption, particularly credit card debt, or debt for any item that depreciates in value. Accumulate and pay cash for all cars, boats, vacations and major household purchases if possible. Reasonable levels of mortgage debt are acceptable, since a place to live is a necessity and not discretionary. However, if you get a mortgage, make sure you have a wide safety margin so you can afford the monthly payments; constantly assess the security of your current income stream. Interest on debt for investments is typically tax-deductible. Contact a good accountant to find out more.

Ignore the Ridicule that Will Come from Being Frugal. We live in a high consumption society, and you may be ostracized and ridiculed for being frugal. Wear it like a badge of honor. Ignore everyone else, knowing that you are taking care of yourself and your family over a lifetime. This is not easy to do, as it requires mental fortitude, courage and a very thick skin. Ultimately, you will have the last laugh.

ACTIONS FOR TRACTION

Describe the vocabulary you use to talk about money. Is it positive or negative, hopeful or fearful, certain or doubtful?

_____

_____

_____

How would you rate your current level of financial education, on a scale from 1 to 10? How can you improve it?

_____

_____

_____

What is one big thing you can do immediately to go the extra mile and create more value in your job or business?

_____

_____

_____

How many passive income streams do you have now, and what is one more you can set up this year?

_____

_____

_____

CHAPTER 13

STAYING HEALTHY AND CONTENT

"Happiness is not something ready-made. It comes from your own actions." | Dalai Lama

MY STORY: MEANWHILE, BACK AT THE RANCH

It was never my personal goal to be happy; rather, I always strove to be content. I viewed the pursuit of happiness as too self-centered and disconnected from progress and, quite frankly, too easy to achieve. Contentment, on the other hand, appealed to my desire for self-reliance, progress, freedom and accomplishment. I am most content when I am progressing.

In 2010, after I had finished my role as President and COO of Powertech Labs, I decided it would be my last executive role. The decision to permanently leave the corporate world as an executive was driven largely by my desire for greater liberty, personal transformation and progress, and therefore more contentment. I saw the arc of my career moving from the early learning phase, to sharing what I had learned, and finally to a focus on health and building a family legacy.

My focus on personal health and family are interconnected, as I believe that one cannot be good to one's family if one is not good to oneself first. The level of mental, physical, spiritual and emotional health required to both survive and thrive in this world is considerable, and needs constant daily attention. I thought long and hard about how I could achieve consistently good health. I did not like the idea of having to commit myself to a significant occupational change purely for health reasons. However, I did want to do something meaningful and enjoyable to complement my work, improve my health and contribute toward a family legacy.

I have always loved the outdoors and the restorative effect of nature. I also loved the idea of owning land, perhaps influenced by the strong emotion I felt reading *The Apprenticeship of Duddy Kravitz* (André Deutsch, 1959), by Mordecai Richler, in high school. It also could have been the influence of growing up in Alberta. Who knows!

Earlier, my wife and I had bought an acreage in the beautiful Nicola Valley near the world-famous Douglas Lake Ranch, and now was the time to enjoy it. It was an old ranch, homesteaded in 1891, located on the eastern slopes of the Cascade Mountains. We knew that owning it would be hard work because the property required a lot of maintenance. However, to me, taking down trees, clearing roads and building fences is not work. It's invigorating exercise and progress: contentment combined with solitude. I enjoy the time there, as a peaceful place to overcome difficulty, build reserves, think creatively and solve problems.

Our modern society is permanently connected, which may cause unnecessary distractions, irritations and superfluous minutiae that drain us of precious energy, time and focus. My experience with our ranch in the mountains has taught me that good health is achieved through daily attention to what is most important: exercise, healthy habits, inner peace and satisfaction with a job well done, while simultaneously and purposely ignoring the energy-sucking distractions of life.

The great accomplishments of my life have been, without a doubt, the most difficult to achieve, but have generated the greatest amount of contentment. Nature and the great outdoors have taught me one enduring lesson: *we are defined by our effort to accomplish, to progress, to move forward and overcome great hardships. The ultimate prize goes to those who endure, who see beauty and wisdom in the struggle, and contentment in the progress.*

HABIT 90

SLEEP WELL

"Light be the earth upon you, lightly rest." | Euripides

It is essential to determine your optimal sleep level and achieve it regularly. This is likely in the range of six to nine hours per night; you know your body best. You should be able to wake up relatively easily each day. Some studies suggest that sleep deprivation is associated with weight gain and obesity, which is one more reason to get your sleep!

The following actions will help you optimize both the quantity and quality of your sleep:

Turn Off Your Screens at Least One Hour Before Bedtime. Artificial light stimulates you and diminishes your subsequent quality of sleep. Replace screen time with reading in bed, preferably a calm and relaxing book.

Keep Your Bedroom Dark, Cool and Well-Ventilated. This will enable deeper, more relaxed breathing and facilitate a better sleep experience. During the summer, run fans to circulate the air and wear a sleep mask to reduce the amount of light.

Stick to a Sleep Routine. Get up at the same time each day, no matter what time you went to bed the night before. This will help you self-regulate, forcing you to go to bed earlier the next night if tired, since you know that you have to get up at the same time the next day.

Get Up Immediately When Your Alarm Goes Off. Wear comfortable and warm sleep clothes so it's easier to get out of bed. Get moving right away, and follow a morning routine for the first 15 minutes so you are on autopilot and don't have to think about it so much.

Avoid Caffeine and Alcohol Before Bed. These two substances will wreak havoc with your deep sleep. Find your personal caffeine cutoff time. Alcohol will dehydrate you, so you will likely drink more water right before bed; you then will need to get up to go to the bathroom, which further disrupts your sleep. If you are at a business function, ask for decaffeinated coffee or tea, and go easy on the alcoholic drinks.

Avoid Strenuous Exercise One to Two Hours Before You Go to Bed. Exercise is a stimulant, and you will have more energy than you need if you are trying to settle for the night. Try to allow at least a few hours of winding down after you complete your workout and post-workout shower. Vigorous exercise in the morning or during the day will improve your sleep quality dramatically, especially if it is done outside, where exposure to fresh air and a variety of weather conditions will boost your immune system.

Allow your mind to rest and replenish. Focus on removing any sources of anxiety and worry so your mind can enter a state of deep relaxation. A settled mind is a settled body.

Sleep deprivation will accumulate over time, and like running a deficit, will build until paid down. Even 15 minutes of shortened sleep each night will accumulate to almost a two-hour shortfall over the course of the week, putting you in an impaired state. This explains why many people sleep in on the weekend. This condition is particularly dangerous for those on shift work, those who travel extensively through different time zones, or anyone who is unable to maintain good daily sleep management techniques.

HABIT 91

MAINTAIN PEAK PHYSICAL CONDITION THROUGH DAILY EXERCISE

"If the wind will not serve, take to the oars." | Latin proverb

In the digital age, where many of us spend the day sitting in front of a computer screen, the importance of regular, sustained, vigorous physical exercise cannot be overstated. Sitting is the new smoking. Living in our modern world does not require much physical hardship. It places little demands on our body, so it is vital to exercise every single day. You will feel sharper overall, your body will be toned, and your mind will be functioning at its optimal level.

Exercise improves blood flow to all your vital organs, especially your brain, and is associated with building mental toughness. This means that regular, vigorous exercise plays a strong part in building up your resilience, allowing you to deal with challenging life events, which we all have. Recent studies have shown there is a direct relationship between exercise and resilience. Furthermore, people who exercise regularly tend to have two to three times higher levels of a crucial protein called brain-derived neurotropic factor (BDNF), compared with people who are sedentary, which is important since low levels of BDNF are linked to dementia.

Vigorous exercise can include brisk walking, running, skiing, cycling, swimming, hiking, cross-training and stationary rowing, for example. Try listening to uplifting and energetic music while exercising. Your mood will lift, and you will want to exercise more. This becomes an important positive feedback loop.

You do not have to do all your exercise in one large chunk, either. Feel free to break up your movement into 10- or 20-minute segments. After a short break from work, you will feel refreshed and actually perform better than if you had simply toughed it out for hours on end. You may have to set an alarm to remind you that is time for that break. Do not feel guilty; it is impossible to give, and give, and give to something or someone else without recharging your battery.

Exercise will recharge your body and mind, and when done on a regular basis, will prevent numerous health problems that are more likely to occur if you are overweight and stressed. This part of your life is as important as brushing, flossing your teeth and maintaining good personal hygiene.

HABIT 92

EAT POWER FOODS FOR A POWER BODY

"Let food be thy medicine and medicine be thy food." | Hippocrates

Developing good eating habits will ensure you have the energy and vitality necessary to live a long life. Get into, and stay in, the habit of eating for nutrition, not for entertainment, since it is crucial that you feed your body the nutrients it needs every single day. Your body and brain are complex machines, so whatever you put in will significantly influence the output.

Here are some food habits to keep you healthy:

Pack Healthy Food. Each night, you should pack a bag for work with enough water, juice, fruit, vegetables, protein and carbohydrates to more than carry you through the next day. The worst thing in the world is to be hungry with only a vending machine nearby.

Eat Small Meals Often. It is better for the human body to eat small meals frequently, to keep blood sugar fairly constant. Think about the last time you felt light-headed or cranky due to lack of food. Apples and bananas work miracles in these situations, and you should never be without them.

Don't Go to Bed Too Full. How about those large meals late at night? Bad idea. Your digestive system needs to wind down at night, too. Give yourself at least two or three hours to fully digest a meal before starting to settle down at night. You will sleep better if your stomach is comfortable and not working hard to process a plateful of food. The reverse is true, too. If you are hungry enough that you can hear your stomach growling, then by all means, go and have that banana or a few light crackers. These are easily digested by most people. You do not want too many deviations on either side of feeling comfortable; make sure you are not too full and not too hungry.

Take Your Vitamins. Vitamin supplements are another item that warrants attention. Malnutrition in any form has been implicated in many mental health disorders and has a significant impact on personal, social and economic success. If you feel sluggish or weak despite doing everything right, it is always a good idea to see a healthcare provider to have your blood work checked. You may have a metabolic imbalance that needs intervention.

A basic multivitamin should be part of your daily nutrition plan, along with other supplements catered to your specific diet. For example, in colder climates during winter months, many people benefit from regular vitamin C and zinc supplements.

BUILD THE BRAIN HEALTH NECESSARY TO LAST A LIFETIME

"The brain is like a muscle. When it is in use we feel very good. Understanding is joyous." | Carl Sagan

The human brain is developed for complex, higher-order thinking; it needs proper care and attention. Your brain will continue to make new neurons throughout your life in response to stimulating mental activity. To do this, you must care for your brain as you do the rest of your body.

Since the brain is about 75% water, you need to stay well-hydrated at all times. You also need to fuel your brain with the right foods. For instance, there is some evidence to suggest that the consumption of seafood is associated with a lower incidence of dementia later in life. Do you want to be independent and fully able to enjoy life into your 90s? Or do you want to be in a care home because you cannot remember how to make porridge for breakfast or how to get from point A to B? Help yourself now by maintaining a healthy brain.

Here are some ways to keep your brain active:

Become Multilingual. People who speak two or more languages have denser gray matter than unilingual people.

Get Enough Sleep. This is especially true if you have been traveling. Jet lag impairs memory, due to the release of stress hormones, so try to catch up on sleep as soon as you can after being in another time zone.

Laugh. Five regions of your brain are activated every time you laugh, so go ahead and watch the occasional funny clip on YouTube. It will do you a lot of good.

Take Up Music. Learning to play any instrument and being able to read music exercises several brain areas at once, and helps develop memory and coordination. Some of the world's greatest musicians live well into their 80s without a hint of dementia.

Keep Learning. Taking any type of continuing education course will also keep your brain sharp. Many of the world's top universities offer free online courses. You can study anything from archaeology to vector calculus.

Get Exercise. In general, an activity that is good for your heart is good for your brain. Aerobic activity, such as running, boosts the oxygen supply to your brain and improves overall learning capacity and memory. Furthermore, running reduces stress hormones, has an antidepressant effect and helps the brain grow new neuronal connections.

No matter what you do, keep your brain healthy, do it regularly, and do it often!

HABIT 94

GIVE IT YOUR BEST EFFORT AND THEN LET IT STAND

"When I stand before God at the end of my life, I would hope that I would not have a single bit of talent left and could say, I used everything you gave me." | Erma Bombeck

Coach John Wooden knows how to lead a team to victory. His UCLA teams hold important National Collegiate Athletic Association (NCAA) records for men's college basketball, including the most national titles (10) and the most consecutive wins (7). Coach Wooden's philosophy was based on one principle: *give a task your absolute best effort, and let it stand.*

In other words, having done your absolute best to complete a task, not only thinking or hoping but knowing in your heart of hearts that you have absolutely done everything you possibly can, let it stand because you can do no more.

Arnold Schwarzenegger adopted the same philosophy on his way to achieving multiple victories, including winning the bodybuilding title of Mr. Universe at age 20, winning the title of Mr. Olympia five times, becoming a Hollywood movie star, becoming a successful businessperson and then being elected governor of the state of California.

In his 1977 docudrama *Pumping Iron,* he stated:

> '*If you want to be a champion, you cannot have any sort of outside negative force affect you. Let's say before the day of a competition I get emotionally involved with a girl. It can have a negative effect on my mind and therefore destroy my workouts. Therefore, I have to cut my emotions off and be, kinda cold, in a way, before competitions. That's what you do with the rest of the things. If someone steals my car from right outside my door right now, I don't care. I couldn't be bothered with it. The only thing I would do is have the secretary call the insurance agent and then laugh about it. Because I cannot be bothered because I have trained for that and not have these things go into my mind.*"

We are often unnecessarily hypercritical of ourselves. This usually happens as a result of knowing that we really did not put our heart into the task at hand; we have disappointed ourselves. The best way to avoid that feeling is to give important tasks your absolute best. Operate at your highest possible standard with the greatest level of effort and excellence, in order to complete it 100%. When that is done, you have left everything on the playing field and you cannot give any more, so do not doubt yourself. Let it stand.

Be true to yourself. You are kidding no one but yourself when you are anything less than 100% truthful about your genuine strengths and weaknesses. It takes courage to face the facts about our own inadequacies, flaws or poor habits. However, it is only through understanding and then ultimately improving these flaws that success will feel more meaningful. Knowing that we stared down our weaknesses and stopped fooling ourselves will bring true courage, accomplishment and a sense of overall happiness: happiness gained from authentic progress by confronting, and overcoming, our inner and greatest fears.

Once you have done your absolute best on a project, do not question yourself anymore. Move on to the next project, proud of your effort, knowing that you have given it your all.

Achieving excellence over a lifetime is a matter of taking steps toward excellence every day. No one can do a lifetime of work in one day. Focus on doing your absolute best in a single day, and let it stand. It's about putting your best foot forward!

HABIT 95

BE AS HAPPY AS YOU DECIDE TO BE

"When one door of happiness closes, another opens, but often we look so long at the closed door that we do not see the one that has been opened for us." | Helen Keller

Happiness plays an important role in the social and emotional bonds we enjoy each day. It is helpful in getting us through a tough time, and can make a significant, positive impact on our friends and families. It causes us to live a more fulfilling, successful life, one filled with joy.

I believe happiness is largely related to our perceptions of our self-image. It is also a result of how we shape our environment, and how we shape ourselves to create happiness in our lives. I believe we literally have the ability to be as happy as we decide to be. While there is increasing evidence of the role of genetics in happiness, it is largely within our control.

If some people decide to live in a funk, whether they have reasons to or not, they live unhappy lives. In some cases, they do not have a reason to be unhappy: they got into the habit of unhappiness. Other people, who have many reasons to be unhappy—usually related to some significant and genuine problem—live joyful lives. They do not have the circumstances to justify it, but it comes from within.

Start by defining happiness in terms of what make sense for you, then do the following to make it happen:

Learn How to Activate Your Happy State. This is easier than it sounds. How many times have you been at home, perhaps in a funk, when the phone or the doorbell rings and you immediately change your mood to be more enthusiastic or outgoing? We can switch ourselves on and off, as there are a series of triggers that can make that happen.

Find Out What Triggers Happiness and Control It. Avoid the triggers that make you unhappy and stressed, and gravitate to the triggers that make you happy. Happiness triggers may be a certain type of music, person, book or exercise. Find out what your happiness triggers are and use them to your advantage.

Surround Yourself with the Environment and People Who Generate Happiness. Certain people bring out the best in us, and other people bring out the worst. To improve our own happiness, it is important that we find those people who bring out the best and develop our relationships with them.

Make Happiness Your Personal Responsibility. If you are a businessperson and you are coming home at the end of a long, stressful day, do not take out your stress on your family. They are not responsible for your day, and they are certainly not responsible for your reaction to your day. If you need to stop somewhere for half an hour, unwind, go for a walk or have a cup of coffee, do so. Have the courage to make happiness something that you are responsible for, and do not take it out on others.

Be Aware of the Long-Term Impacts of Happiness. Prolonged periods of depression or stress can cause significant emotional damage, not only to you: they can also lead to breakups and damage in a family. Take up being happy as a duty. Find those triggers, find those people, find that environment and generate that happiness on a daily basis.

HABIT 96

CONTRIBUTE YOUR UNIQUE GIFTS

"How wonderful it is that nobody need wait a single moment before starting to improve the world." | Anne Frank

Each of us has unique gifts. These special gifts are often disguised in a way that makes it very difficult to find them. Sometimes they even come disguised as obstacles, problems or difficulties. Our gifts can be intellectual, artistic or emotional, and they are one special way we can contribute. However, we are often surrounded by people who do not look for our gifts; therefore, we are not encouraged to look for them either. *Find out what your gifts are and determine how best to start contributing to society.*

The best way to find your gifts is to take some time to truly understand your own natural skills. Listen to what other people say when they give you feedback about what you're doing well, what they like about you and what is unique about you. Do not downplay their compliments and put yourself down; there are enough people willing to do that for you. Let the people complimenting you lift you up. This feedback will be helpful.

Once you identify your unique gifts, start moving in that direction.

It may not be your job, it may not even be a hobby, but it may be something you can do to make the world a better place. Maybe it is singing in the church choir on the weekend, or coaching your son's or daughter's basketball team. Whatever it is, find that gift in you and start contributing it in any way you can.

Sometimes our gifts are revealed through trouble, trauma or even tragedy. I have seen incredibly good acts come from very tragic circumstances. For example, Mothers Against Drunk Driving (MADD) was founded when Candace Lightner's 13-year-old daughter Cari was killed by a drunk hit-and-run driver repeat offender. MADD's dogged persistence is credited with helping to reduce the incidents of drunk driving by 50% since 1980.

Find your unique gifts and contribute to help others. If you do this on a regular basis, you will form a habit, and make yourself better every day.

HABIT 97

BUILD LONG-TERM, WARM RELATIONSHIPS

"I've learned that people will forget what you said, people will forget what you did, but people will never forget how you made them feel." | Maya Angelou

The Harvard Grant Study followed 268 male Harvard undergraduates from the class of 1938–1940 for 75 years, collecting data on various aspects of their lives. Researchers wanted to answer the age-old question "What is the key to happiness?" *One of the study's most important findings is that the key to happiness is loving, supportive and warm relationships.*

Over the course of your life, your social circle, including your family, friends and colleagues, will lift you up when times are bad, share the load when times are hard, and celebrate when times are good. These relationships are the ones that will define your life, make you happy and fulfilled, and bring out the best in you.

Here are some steps to nurturing strong, loving relationships in your life:

Put in the Effort. Get into the daily habit of maintaining warm relationships with those you care for most, particularly your family, friends and workmates. Think of relationships in terms of decades or a lifetime, and then the little day-to-day problems will soon disappear. By putting in the effort, you become bigger than yourself, and the relationship will pay dividends for both you and your friend for many years into the future.

Take the Initiative. Call people regularly. Remember them on their birthdays and at special times of the year. Thank them for the things they have done for you, and call them when you know they are feeling down. Make a point of being the one to call them, rather than trying to get the upper hand by having them call you.

Reciprocate. No one will give indefinitely to a one-way relationship. When someone reaches out to you, reciprocate. Don't expect reciprocation back all the time (in fact, rarely expect it), but make a point of reciprocating when others are kind to you. Be there for others when they call you; try to look beyond the vicissitudes and tribulations of daily life.

The continuous and daily improvements in the quality of the important relationships is one of the biggest opportunities for long-term satisfaction and impact. It is truly the gift that keeps on giving. The more we put into long-term and warm relationships, the more we get out of them and the more we want to give.

Make it a habit to say a few kind words each day to your friends and family. Call a friend periodically and offer to help. Make your workmates feel important, and let them know you care. You may be surprised with how far these small acts of kindness and consideration go.

HABIT 98

START BUILDING YOUR LEGACY TODAY

"Our days are numbered. One of the primary goals in our lives should be to prepare for our last day. The legacy we leave is not just in our possessions, but in the quality of our lives." | Billy Graham

Contentment comes from knowing we have tried our best and made a difference. As we grow older and come to the second half of our lives, it is natural to start looking back over what we have done, the difference we have made for ourselves, our family and our community.

Don't wait too long to see what you have left. Start defining your legacy today. Start to think about what is important and how you want to be remembered: a successful businessperson, academic, leader or doctor, or a good parent. Once you have defined it, clarify it and immediately work toward building it.

A legacy takes time to build, but each one of us has the capacity to make a significant, memorable contribution to society. This realization will make you more content while you are defining your legacy and planning the final decades of your life. Knowing that you have made a difference will give your life meaning while giving you motivation to contribute more.

Here is how you can start building your legacy today:

Plan for the Inevitable. There is no question about it: each one of us is going to die someday. There is no use in hiding from it and leaving your family with a mess when you are gone. Show some courage and plan for your graceful end. *Make an estate plan, create a will, clear your debts and get all your paperwork in order.*

Do It Now. No use in waiting to do the things you always wanted to do: you might as well do them right now. I am not talking about being fiscally irresponsible; just immediately take action, no matter how small, on things that are important to you. Contribute to a charity, start a foundation, help a family member: all of these are ways to build an enduring legacy.

Tell People You Love Them. Your legacy building can start today by telling those people most important to you that you love them and care for them deeply. Not only will this help build a stronger legacy for you, but the very act will likely bring you peace of mind and help your own longevity.

Help Your Next Generation. The foundation of your legacy can be established and then strengthened by helping the next generation. Leave a legacy that keeps on giving, like a multigenerational family business. Not only can you provide financially for future generations, for which your children will certainly be appreciative, but you can embed your values and character into future generations, magnifying your impact.

HABIT 99

TRANSITION, TRANSFORM AND GROW

"Fall seven times and stand up eight." | Japanese proverb

The human condition is progress, accomplishment and achievement, not stagnation or maintaining the status quo. This has enabled the human race to evolve dramatically, so we were not shaped by the world, but instead, we would shape the world around us. We must always transition, transform and grow. Even a lion, the king of the beasts, wakes up every day and must move in order to hunt and survive. Likewise, all of us must wake up every day and put forth our best efforts in order to improve ourselves.

The world we live in is changing rapidly. Technology, globalization and the shrinking the middle class means that the old institutions are falling fast and new ones are developing, changing our world every day. Those who do not change will soon be left behind.

In the past, you were left behind over the course of a generation, and then decades. Now, one can be left behind in the course of years. It becomes imperative to transform on an ongoing, regular basis.

Here are the best ways to do this:

Let Go of All Fear, Pride and Resentment. These emotions are holding you back from being the type of person you are meant to be, both professionally and personally. Let these emotions go, take more risks and associate with different people. This puts your transformation back in your own hands, so it is not left to the whim of change and society.

Stop Talking About the Past. Nobody wants to hear about what happened 20 years ago. Nobody wants to hear about what you did in high school or what you could have done if things had been different. Your friends or children may listen respectfully, but they really do not want to hear it either. Only focus on the present.

Be Fearful of Backsliding. Be concerned about being left behind, as this will motivate you to make dramatic changes in your life. Don't constantly live in fear, but rather be fearful of inaction, the status quo, or irrelevance.

Find Good Role Models. Look for examples of other people who have transformed their lives and learn from them:

- *Cal Ripken, Jr.*, the Iron Man, set the record for the highest number of consecutive baseball games played (2,632) and then transformed himself into a world-class author.

- *George Foreman* finished his boxing career broke and then proceeded to make over $100 million on his idea for a better grill to cook hamburgers (which he loved).

- *U2*, the Irish rock band, started in 1981 and aggressively transformed themselves to appeal to a younger generation, building a whole new market and a demographic that keeps them going today.

Find those kinds of people, learn from what they did and apply it to your own life.

HABIT 100

NEVER RETIRE

"It does not matter how slowly you go as long as you do not stop." | Confucius

Retirement is an invention of the modern era. Prior to 1883, the concept of retirement did not exist, and people worked until they could not work any longer. In 1883, Chancellor Otto Von Bismarck of Germany decided to pay pensions to any non-working German over the age 65, largely to appease the population in a self-serving political effort to maintain control and offset the promises made by his socialist political opponents. At that time, the average life expectancy was 62, so he had come up with the scheme that, while very appealing, most people would never be able to take advantage of.

Today, most of us live much longer and age 65 has become the de facto standard for retirement. Most 65-year-olds today are not only capable of working, but are interested in working and, more importantly, have accumulated a lifetime of valuable expertise, skills and knowledge.

The concept of retirement, or stopping work, has been shown to have negative health effects. There is evidence that some people, after working and retiring, diminish their health or even die prematurely.

Retirement is an outdated, anachronistic concept that is completely unfitting with the digital age we live in. Retirement can literally kill you, at a time in life where you have the maximum to contribute.

If you embrace the concept of *The 1% Solution*, that you need to improve a little each day in order to make a significant change over a lifetime, age 65 will be no different than any other year for you. You will evolve, change and improve your life in a manner consistent with your goals and objectives, regardless of your age. If you are able to accumulate a pension at age 65, that is a financial tactical matter, not a career or life question.

In terms of lifestyle, you should be looking to contribute more as you get older, and help yourself, your family and your community as much as you are able. I believe we each have an obligation to commit to the best of our abilities in order to live a fulfilled life.

If you have worked a long, hard life, and decide to do something different, go for it. Keep in mind that a life of idleness and leisure will be unhealthy, financially risky and set a poor example for those who look up to you.

Replace the concept of retirement with the concept of rejuvenation or reinvention, and start transitioning from work you are compelled to do to work you are called to do.

Start this process well in advance, perhaps decades prior. Build the skill set necessary for your future work by taking courses, going back to school or starting to turn your avocation into a job.

If you have children, consider starting a multigenerational project that you will not be able to complete in your lifetime, like building a substantial business. This will not only give you the motivation you need to work well past 65, but it will also provide you with a worthwhile project that will keep you sharp, skilled and contributing.

Reduce the time you spend with anyone in your life who is becoming excessively idle in retirement. Excessive downtime causes a person to spend more and get less exercise, and can have serious detrimental effects on health. Stay focused on being around super active people who have taken on big and challenging projects, and want to keep themselves extraordinarily busy.

Never retire, never take your foot off the accelerator and never quit!

ACTIONS FOR TRACTION

How would you rate the quality of your sleep (1–10), and what steps can to take to improve it?

_____

_____

_____

List three ways to keep your brain healthy. Start at least one today.

_____

_____

_____

What triggers happiness for you and how can you do more of it?

_____

_____

_____

If you wrote your own eulogy now, what would it be? Are you satisfied with it? If not, write what you would like it to be and how you want to be remembered.

_____

_____

_____

CONCLUSION

Life is a marathon, not a sprint, so plan for the long term. *The 1% Solution* is a mindset that will help you build the good habits necessary to get you across the finish line of your own personal marathon.

If you are struggling with discipline and want to improve your habits, start with a big sigh of relief as you finish reading this book. Don't be too hard on yourself for having flaws: everyone does. Instead, concentrate on the fact that you are actually trying to do something about it. This puts you in a very small and select group of people. If you hold on to the thought that you are a bad person because you have bad habits, you will attract more of those thoughts into your life, and more bad habits. Forgive yourself entirely and move on toward improvement.

Start by putting your time scale into perspective. No mere mortal achieves a state of perfection, grace and habitual goodness; instead, we strive for perfection over our lifetimes. Give yourself plenty of time to make improvements and remind yourself that you will never be perfect, although you can continually strive to be better.

Make the distinction between human nature and habits. There is very little we can do to change human nature, since much of it is biological or evolutionary and meant for our own protection. For instance, it is human nature to feel a fight-or-flight response to certain threats.

We are evolutionarily driven to eat when food is available, since our body does not know if food will be scarce or plentiful. Habits can moderate or improve human nature, but cannot replace it.

Treating your habit development as a lifelong improvement project will give you a sense of perspective. However, don't become complacent, since the difference between daily improvement and daily decline can be very small, or even imperceptible.

I believe we have an obligation to stay true to our mission of self-improvement, so we can progress to a higher state of character and become complete human beings. By seeking goodness and improvement we can contribute more to the world in the short time we have and, hopefully, leave it a bit better than the way we found it. If enough people take this attitude and focus on improving themselves, rather than trying to improve those around them, then I am sure we will achieve more as individuals and progress more as a people.

Be great and let your light shine for all the world to see.

Eamonn Percy

ONE WAY TO PERMANENTLY CHANGE HABITS

A number of years ago, during my study of successful people, I read several biographies of Benjamin Franklin. I must admit that I was skeptical about Franklin at first, largely out of ignorance, since I only had a superficial understanding of his life, and had not appreciated the significant impact he had on American history. Subsequently, I was amazed to read about how the youngest son of 17 children started working at 12 years of age, and was independently wealthy 28 years later at age 40. He went on to be a prolific inventor, established the first US hospital, postal system, sanitary system and school system, and was pivotal in establishing the entire country as a Founding Father! While there is no doubt that he was gifted, he did suffer from the occasional discipline lapse and decided to embark on a lifelong journey of seeking moral perfection through habit improvement.

He realized that the achievement of a worthwhile goal, including wealth building, required the highest moral standing and the attainment of virtue. He also knew that building virtue and integrity required constant daily attention, so he embarked on a system of habit building, as described in his autobiography, *Memoirs*, written from 1771 to 1790, as follows:

> *"It was about this time I conceived the bold and arduous project of arriving at moral perfection. I wished to live without committing any fault at any time; I would conquer all that either natural inclination, custom, or company might lead me into. As I knew, or thought I knew, what was right and wrong, I did not see why I might not always do the one and avoid the other. But I soon found I had undertaken a task of more difficulty than I had imagined. While my care was employed in guarding against one fault, I was often surprised by another; habit took the advantage of inattention; inclination was sometimes too strong for reason. I concluded, at length, that the mere speculative conviction that it was our interest to be completely virtuous was not sufficient to prevent our slipping, and that the contrary habits must be broken, and good ones acquired and established, before we can have any dependence on a steady, uniform rectitude of conduct. For this purpose I therefore contrived the following method.*
>
> *In the various enumerations of the moral virtues I met in my reading, I found the catalogue more or less numerous, as different writers included more or fewer ideas under the same name. Temperance, for example, was by some confined to eating and drinking, while by others it was extended to mean the moderating every other pleasure, appetite, inclination, or passion, bodily or mental, even to our avarice and ambition. I proposed to myself, for the sake of clearness, to use rather more names, with fewer ideas annexed to each, than a few names with more ideas; and I included under thirteen names of virtues all that at that time occurred to*

me as necessary or desirable, and annexed to each a short precept, which fully expressed the extent I gave to its meaning.

These names of virtues, with their precepts were:

Temperance
Eat not to dullness; drink not to elevation.

Silence
Speak not but what may benefit others or yourself; avoid trifling conversation.

Order
Let all your things have their places; let each part of your business have its time.

Resolution
Resolve to perform what you ought; perform without fail what you resolve.

Frugality
Make no expense but to do good to others or yourself, i.e., waste nothing.

Industry
Lose no time; be always employed in something useful; cut off all unnecessary actions.

Sincerity
Use no hurtful deceit; think innocently and justly, and, if you speak, speak accordingly.

Justice
Wrong none by doing injuries or omitting the benefits that are your duty.

Moderation
Avoid extremes; forbear resenting injuries so much as you think they deserve.

Cleanliness
Tolerate no uncleanliness in body, clothes, or habitation.

Tranquility
Be not disturbed at trifles, or at accidents common or unavoidable.

Chastity
Rarely use venery but for health or offspring, never to dullness, weakness, or the injury of your own or another's peace or reputation.

Humility
Imitate Jesus and Socrates.

My intention being to acquire the habitude of all these virtues, I judged it would be well not to distract my attention by attempting the whole at once, but to fix it on one of them at a time, and, when I should be master of that, then to proceed to another, and so on, till I should have gone thro' the thirteen; and, as the previous acquisition of some might facilitate the acquisition of certain others, I arranged them with that view, as they stand above. Temperance first, as it tends to procure that coolness and clearness of head which is so necessary where constant vigilance was to be kept up, and guard maintained against the unremitting attraction of ancient habits and the force of perpetual temptations. This being acquired and established, Silence would be more easy; and my desire being to gain knowledge at the same time that

I improved in virtue, and considering that in conversation it was obtained rather by the use of the ears than of the tongue, and therefore wishing to break a habit I was getting into prattling, punning, and joking, which only made me acceptable to trifling company, I gave Silence the second place. This and the next, Order, I expected would allow me more time for attending to my project and my studies. Resolution, once because habitual, would keep me firm in my endeavors to obtain all the subsequent virtues; Frugality and Industry, freeing me from my remaining debt, and producing affluence and independence, would make more easy the practice of Sincerity and Justice, etc., Conceiving, then, that, agreeably to the advice of Pythagoras in his Garden Verses, daily examination would be necessary, I contrived the following method for conducting that examination.

I made a little book, in which I allotted a page for each of the virtues. I ruled each page with red ink, so as to have seven columns, one for each day of the week, marking each column with a letter for the day. I crossed these columns with thirteen red lines, marking the beginning of each line with the first letter of one of the virtues, on which line, and in its proper column, I might mark, by a little black spot, every fault I found upon examination to have been committed respecting that virtue upon that day.

TEMPERANCE

EAT NOT TO DULLNESS; DRINK NOT TO ELEVATION.

	S	M	T	W	T	F	S
Temperance							
Silence	**	*		*		*	
Order	*	*	*		*	*	*
Resolution			*		*		
Frugality		*			*		
Industry			*				
Sincerity							
Justice							
Moderation							
Cleanliness							
Tranquility							
Chastity							
Humility							

I determined to give a week's strict attention to each of the virtues successively. Thus, in the first week, my great guard was to avoid every the least offense against Temperance, leaving the other virtues to their ordinary chance, only marking every evening the faults of the day. Thus, if in the first week I could keep my first line, marked T, clear of spots, I supposed the habit of that virtue so much strengthened, and its opposite weakened, that I might venture extending my attention to include the next, and for the following week keep both lines clear of spots. Proceeding thus to the last, I could go thro' a course complete in thirteen weeks, and four courses in a years. And like him who, having a garden to weed, does not attempt to eradicate all the bad herbs at once, which would exceed his reach and his strength, but works on one of the beds at a time, and, having accomplished the first, proceeds to a second, so I should have, I hoped, the encouraging pleasure of seeing on my pages the progress I made in virtue, by clearing successively my lines of their spots, till in the end, by a number of courses, I should be happy in viewing a clean book, after a thirteen weeks' daily examination.

This my little book had for its motto these lines from Addison's "Cato":

Here will I hold. If there's a power above us (And that there is, all nature cries aloud Thro' all her works), He must delight in virtue; And that which He delights in must be happy."

I adopted this system myself several years ago and have found it to be the best method I have come across to improve my own habits. It is easy to implement, requires no cost, and gracefully allows failure since the focus is on seeking perfection, not on being perfect itself. I made modifications to the system by adding my own *Wealth Building* and *Health Habits*.

This is the best system I know to improve habits and, in the absence of another system, I recommend you give it a try.

There are other good accountability systems as well, such as a good marriage, good business partners, good family businesses, *Mastermind* groups, teams, coaches and community groups. Find the one that works best for you and stick with it.

A quick word on your environment. Some people have the good fortune of being in a cultural, family or work environment that promotes good habits. If you are one of these fortunate people, cherish what you have and be thankful that you have a natural, built-in social accountability system that is helping you get better each day.

If you don't feel that your environment is conducive to good habit-building, I strongly urge you to consider changing it dramatically and fast. Outside of the accountability systems I mentioned previously, your environment is the next most important factor that will help you build good habits and prevent backsliding.

For instance, it is very difficult, if not impossible, to quit smoking if you work or live with heavy smokers. Some people have done it, but the close and regular proximity to other smokers makes relapse a much higher likelihood. If this is your case and quitting smoking is important, get a transfer or quit your job. Conversely, if developing the habits of wealth-building is important to you, then being in an environment of other wealth-builders on a daily basis will dramatically increase your probability of success.

This combination of a daily accountability system, complemented by a supportive and conducive environment, is the best way I know to develop good habits.

The goal is to prevent relapses into bad habits, while rewarding good habits on a daily basis. The cumulative effect of these two actions compounds, like money in the bank, to provide a rich reward for you and your family in the future.

WHAT TO DO NEXT

Thank you for reading this book!

Before you put this book away, make it count and decide to take some action immediately to improve your habits. Don't wait. Take action now to make your life better.

Here are some suggestions. Pick one and start today!

- Discuss this book with your partner, a close friend or family member, and ask him or her to suggest one habit you should work on to improve over the next 30 days.

- Share *The 1% Solution* with a friend or colleague, and discuss it.

- Pick one habit and concentrate on improving it each day for a week.

- Start a book club and discuss *The 1% Solution*.

- Start a *1% Solution Mastermind* with five close friends for support.

- Start a *1% Solution* Facebook group and invite your friends to join.

Taking some form of action immediately after reading this book will reinforce the behaviors of good habits, and increase the likelihood that you will successfully make permanent changes in your life.

RECOMMENDED
ADDITIONAL RESOURCES

CHAPTER 1: A STRONG FOUNDATION

Dweck, Carol S., *Mindset: The New Psychology of Success* (New York, 2006)

Maltz, Maxwell, *Psycho-Cybernetics: A New Way to Get More Living out of Life* (Englewood Cliffs, 1960)

Ziglar, Zig, *See You at the Top* (Petaling Jaya, 1977)

Covey, Stephen R., *The Seven Habits of Highly Effective People: Restoring the Character Ethic* (Melbourne, 1989)

CHAPTER 2: BEING GOOD

Robbins, Anthony, *Awaken the Giant Within: How to Take Immediate Control of Your Mental, Emotional, Physical & Financial Destiny* (New York, 1991)

Goleman, Daniel, *Emotional Intelligence: Why It Can Matter More than IQ* (New York, 1995)

Carnegie, Dale, *How to Win Friends and Influence People* (New York, 1981)

Franklin, Benjamin, *The Autobiography of Benjamin Franklin* (New York, 1996)

CHAPTER 3: ACHIEVING GOALS

Frankl, Viktor Emil, *Man's Search for Meaning* (New York, 1963)

Wallace, B. Alan, *The Attention Revolution: Unlocking the Power of the Focused Mind* (Boston, 2006)

Schwartz, David Joseph, *The Magic of Thinking Big* (New York, 1987)

Peale, Norman Vincent, *The Power of Positive Thinking* (New York, 1952)

Warren, Richard, *The Purpose-Driven Life: What on Earth Am I Here for?* (Grand Rapids, 2002)

CHAPTER 4: OVERCOMING OBSTACLES

Maxwell, John C., *Failing Forward: Turning Mistakes into Stepping-Stones for Success* (Nashville, TN, 2000)

Christiansen, Rich, *The Zigzag Principle: the Goal-Setting Strategy That Will Revolutionize Your Business and Your Life* (New York, 2012)

Kushner, Harold S., *When Bad Things Happen to Good People* (New York, 1981)

Chödrön Pema, *When Things Fall Apart: Heart Advice for Difficult Times* (Boston, 1997)

CHAPTER 5: BUILDING A CAREER

Bettger, Frank, *How I Raised Myself from Failure to Success in Selling* (Englewood Cliffs, 1949)

Gladwell, Malcolm, *Outliers: The Story of Success* (New York, 2008)

Duhigg, Charles, *The Power of Habit: Why We Do What We Do in Life and Business* (New York, 2012)

CHAPTER 6: MANAGING TIME WELL

Bregman, Peter, *18 Minutes: Find Your Focus, Master Distraction, and Get the Right Things Done* (New York, 2011)

Tracy, Brian, *Eat That Frog! : 21 Great Ways to Stop Procrastinating and Get More Done in Less Time* (San Francisco, 2007)

Covey, Stephen R., Rebecca R. Merrill, and A. Rogers Merrill, *First Things First* (London, 1996)

Lakein, Alan, *How to Get Control of Your Time and Your Life* (New York, 1973)

CHAPTER 7: MAKING EFFECTIVE DECISIONS

Maxwell, John C., *How Successful People Think: Change Your Thinking, Change Your Life* (New York, 2009)

Deming, William Edwards, *Out of the Crisis: Quality, Productivity and Competitive Position* (Cambridge, 1988)

Gawande, Atul, *The Checklist Manifesto: How to Get Things Right* (New York, 2010)

Kahneman, Daniel, *Thinking, Fast and Slow* (New York, 2012)

CHAPTER 8: LEARNING TO LEAD

Collins, James C., *Good to Great: Why Some Companies Make the Leap... And Others Don't* (New York, 2001)

Cialdini, Robert B., *Influence: the Psychology of Persuasion* (New York, 2007)

Ferrazzi, Ken, and Tahl Raz, *Never Eat Alone,* (2014)

Goodwin, Doris Kearns, *Team of Rivals: the Political Genius of Abraham Lincoln* (New York, 2006)

Greene, Robert, *The 48 Laws of Power* (London, 2000)

Goman, Carol Kinsey, *The Silent Language of Leaders: How Body Language Can Help-or Hurt-How You Lead* (San Francisco, 2011)

Kouzes, James M., and Barry Z. Posner, *The Truth about Leadership the No-Fads, Heart-of-the-Matter Facts You Need to Know* (San Francisco, 2010)

CHAPTER 9: COMMUNICATING WITH POISE

Patterson, Kerry, *Crucial Conversations: Tools for Talking When Stakes Are High* (New York, 2002)

Maxwell, John C., *Everyone Communicates, Few Connect: What the Most Effective People Do Differently* (Nashville, 2010)

Gallo, Carmine, *Talk like TED: the 9 Public Speaking Secrets of the World's*

Top Minds (New York, 2014)

Carnegie, Dale, and Dorothy Carnegie, *The Quick and Easy Way to Effective Speaking* (New York, 1962)

CHAPTER 10: GETTING THINGS DONE

Bossidy, Larry, Ram Charan, and Charles Burck, *Execution: the Discipline of Getting Things Done* (New York, 2002)

Allen, David, *Getting Things Done: the Art of Stress-Free Productivity* (New York, 2001)

Koch, Richard, *The 80/20 Principle: the Secret of Achieving More with Less* (New York, 1998)

Drucker, Peter F., *Effective Executive: the Definitive Guide to Getting the Right Things* (New York, 2006)

Black, Steven G., *The Four Steps to the Epiphany: Successful Strategies for Products That Win* (2013)

CHAPTER 11: STAYING MOTIVATED

Pink, Daniel H., *Drive: the Surprising Truth about What Motivates Us* (New York, 2009)

Ziglar, Zig, *Developing the Qualities of Success* (Issaquahm, 2016)

Pausch, Randy, and Jeffrey Zaslow, *The Last Lecture* (New York, 2008)

Burchard, Brendon, *The Motivation Manifesto: 9 Declarations to Claim Your Personal Power* (2014)

CHAPTER 12: ACHIEVING FINANCIAL SUCCESS

Siebold, Steve, *How Rich People Think* (Naperville, 2014)

Kiyosaki, Robert T., *Rich Dad, Poor Dad: What the Rich Teach Their Kids about Money—That the Poor and the Middle Class Do Not!* (Paradise Valley, 2009)

O'Leary, Kevin, *Cold Hard Truth on Men, Women & Money: 50 Common Money Mistakes and How to Fix Them* (New York, 2014)

Clason, George S., *The Richest Man in Babylon* (New York, 1955)

Wattles, W. D., *The Science of Getting Rich* (New York, 2007)

Hill, Napoleon, *Think and Grow Rich* (La Vergna, 2009)

CHAPTER 13: STAYING HEALTHY AND CONTENT

Jaminet, Paul, and Shou-Ching Jaminet, *Perfect Health Diet: Regain Health and Lose Weight by Eating the Way You Were Meant to Eat* (New York, 2012)

Dalai Lama and Howard C. Cutler, *The Art of Happiness: a Handbook for Living* (New York, 1998)

Durant, John, and Michael Malice, *The Paleo Manifesto: Ancient Wisdom for Lifelong Health* (New York, 2014)

Tolle, Eckhart, *The Power of Now: a Guide to Spiritual Enlightenment* (Novato, 1999)

QUOTE SOURCE PROFILES

George Addair was the founder of the Omega Vector. Founded in 1978, this Arizona-based self-knowledge program has changed the lives of over 65,000 participants.

Robert G. Allen is an influential investment adviser and the author of many *New York Times* bestselling books (over four million copies sold). Thousands of millionaires attribute their success to him.

Maya Angelou was an African-American author, poet and civil rights activist. Her autobiography *I Know Why the Caged Bird Sings* became a bestseller immediately after publication and has never been out of print.

Aristotle was a Greek philosopher and scientist who made significant contributions to the study of logic, psychology and biology. His views on physical science lasted well over 1,000 years.

St. Augustine was an early Christian theologian and philosopher. He was a prolific author whose writings influenced the development of Western Christianity and Western philosophy.

Francis Bacon was an English philosopher, statesman, scientist, jurist, orator, essayist and author known as the father of the scientific method. He stated that he had three goals: to uncover the truth, to serve his country, and to serve his church.

Alexander Graham Bell was a Scottish-born scientist, inventor, engineer and innovator who is credited with patenting the first practical telephone. He was a founding member of the National Geographic Society and patented 30 inventions (18 in his name alone).

Erma Bombeck was an American humorist who wrote newspaper columns chronicling the life of a midwestern suburban housewife. She authored 15 books (most of them bestsellers) and by the 1970s, her biweekly columns were read by 30 million people.

Edward de Bono is a Maltese physician, psychologist, author, inventor and consultant. He originated the term Lateral Thinking and is a proponent of the teaching of thinking as a subject in schools. His thinking tools have been incorporated into school curriculums in over 20 countries.

Richard Branson is an English billionaire businessman and investor who is best known as the founder of Virgin Group. He started selling records as a student in the 1960s; today, he has a net worth of nearly $5 billion USD.

Buddha was an Indian sage on whose teachings Buddhism was formed, which has approximately 350 million adherents, or 6% of the global population. He spent many decades traveling and teaching people from all walks of life.

Warren Buffett is an American business magnate and philanthropist known as *The Most Successful Investor in the World*, with a net worth of over $63 billion USD.

Dale Carnegie was the author of the bestselling book *How to Win Friends and Influence People*. A course based on his ideas was founded in 1912; today it is offered in over 90 countries and has been completed by over eight million people.

G.K. Chesterton was an English writer, speaker, lay theologian, philosopher, literary and art critic, and Christian Apologist. He delivered popular talks on BBC radio during the 1930s and wrote many works, including books, essays, short stories, poems and plays.

Winston Churchill was the Prime Minister of the United Kingdom during World War II. He won the Nobel Prize for Literature, was rated as one of the most influential leaders by *Time* magazine, and came first in BBC's 2002 poll of 100 Greatest Britons.

Christopher Columbus was an Italian explorer who completed four voyages across the Atlantic Ocean and who is credited with discovering the New World of The Americas.

Confucius was a Chinese philosopher whose morals gave rise to Confucianism. His principles advocated strong family loyalty, ancestor worship, and respect of elders by their children. Today his ideas are followed by over three million people.

Russell H. Conwell was an American Baptist minister, orator, philanthropist, lawyer and writer. He delivered his inspirational essay *Acres of Diamonds* over 6,000 times all over the world.

Stephen Covey is an American author and speaker. He is best known for his book *The Seven Habits of Highly Effective People*, which has sold over 25 million copies in 38 languages. He was named one of *Time* magazine's most influential Americans in 1996.

Marie Curie was a Polish/French scientist who pioneered the study of radioactivity. She was the first woman to win a Nobel Prize, the first person to win two Nobel prizes, and the first woman to become a professor at the University of Paris.

The current **Dalai Lama** is Tenzin Gyatso, a Buddhist monk who won the Nobel Peace Prize in 1989. He is known for his interest in science and his advocacy for Tibetans.

Amelia Earhart was an American aviation pioneer and the first woman to fly solo across the Atlantic Ocean. She disappeared over the Pacific Ocean in 1937. She won multiple awards, wrote multiple books and inspired a generation of female aviators.

Albert Einstein was a German-born theoretical physicist who developed the theory of relativity and the mass-energy equivalence formula. He won the Nobel Prize in Physics, and was named Person of the Century by *Time* magazine in 1999.

Ralph Waldo Emerson was an American essayist, lecturer and poet who led the Transcendentalist movement of the mid-19th century. His works explored the ideas of freedom and individuality. He became the leading voice of intellectual culture in the United States.

Euripides was a tragedian in ancient Greece. He wrote over 90 plays, of which 19 have survived to this day.

Philip Fisher was an American stock investor. He wrote the popular investing guide *Common Stocks and Uncommon Profits*, which has remained in print since it was first published in 1958.

Henry Ford was the founder of the Ford Motor Company and is considered the father of mass production. He pioneered the assembly line technique and created the first affordable car for the middle class. In 1999, he was included on Gallup's list of 18 widely admired people of the 20th century.

Anne Frank was a Jewish German-born diarist in World War II. Her diary, which chronicled her life while in hiding from the Nazis, was published posthumously. In 1999, *Time* magazine listed her as one of the most important people of the century.

Benjamin Franklin was one of the Founding Fathers of the United States. He was a leading author, printer, statesman, inventor and scientist. He earned the title of First American, and his image has been honored on the US $100 bill.

Mahatma Gandhi was an Indian lawyer and civil rights activist, and the leader of the Indian independence movement in British-ruled India. He was named Man of the Year by *Time* magazine in 1930.

Johann Wolfgang von Goethe was a prolific German writer whose works were referenced by famed psychologists, including Freud, and set to music by composers, including Mozart and Beethoven.

Vincent van Gogh was a Dutch Post-Impressionist artist who was famous for his still life paintings and self-portraits. Along with Picasso, his paintings are among the world's most expensive paintings ever sold.

Billy Graham is an American evangelist and was a spiritual adviser to several American presidents.

Hippocrates was a classical Greek physician who is referred to as the Father of Western Medicine. He is credited with writing the Hippocratic Oath, which is still taken today by people entering the field of medicine.

Jesus was the founder of Christianity, which is the world's largest religion today, with an estimated 2.2 billion adherents, representing about 30% of the world's population.

Steve Jobs was the co-founder and CEO of Apple, Inc. Apple's products have had a massive impact on the way people interact with one another and the world around them.

Helen Keller was a blind and deaf American writer, political activist, and lecturer. In 1999, she was listed in Gallup's Most Widely Admired People of the 20th Century.

Stephen King is a prolific American author of horror novels. His books have won over 80 awards and sold over 350 million copies worldwide.

Robert Kiyosaki is an American self-help author and motivational speaker known for his *Rich Dad, Poor Dad* series of books. His books have sold over 26 million copies, and he has a net worth of $80 million.

Abraham Lincoln was the president of the United States during the Civil War. Known as an astute politician and a champion of human liberty, he is consistently ranked by scholars in the top three American presidents in history.

Vince Lombardi was an American football player and one of the top coaches in professional football history. He never had a losing season as a head coach in the NFL.

Harvey Mackay is a businessman, self-help columnist and author of seven *New York Times* bestselling books.

Maimonides was an influential medieval Jewish philosopher, astronomer, Torah scholar, and physician. Several hospitals and universities have been named after him, and Harvard University issued a memorial volume to commemorate the 800th anniversary of his death.

John C. Maxwell is an American author, speaker and pastor who has written many books on leadership. His books have sold millions of copies and made the *New York Times* Best Sellers list. In 2014, *Inc.* magazine named him the top leadership and management expert in the world.

Sakyong Mipham is a leader of a sect of Tibetan Buddhism and the head of Shambhala International.

Sir Claus Moser was a British statistician and academic. He was a life peer in Britain and the recipient of an Order of Merit in Germany, and held positions of authority in a vast number of well-respected institutions including the London Philharmonic Orchestra and the British Museum.

William H. Murray was a Scottish mountain climber and writer. He wrote the first draft of his first book on toilet paper in a prisoner-of-war camp and rewrote it after it was confiscated by the Gestapo.

Earl Nightingale was an American writer, speaker and radio personality who focused on character development, motivation and excellence. His spoken word record *The Strangest Secret* sold over a million copies and was the first spoken word record to gain Gold Record status.

Anaïs Nin was a Cuban-born author who is known for her journals. She was friends with many of the best-known writers in the early 20th century.

Pablo Picasso was a Spanish artist known for co-founding Cubism and collage. Several of his paintings rank among the most expensive paintings in the world.

Plato was a Greek philosopher and mathematician. He, Socrates and Aristotle laid the foundation of Western philosophy and science.

Ayn Rand was a Russian-born writer and philosopher who advocated reason as the only way to gain knowledge. Her books, including *Atlas Shrugged*, have sold over 29 million copies.

Jim Rohn was an American entrepreneur, author and motivational speaker who rose from poverty to a distinguished speaking career. He received an award for excellence in speaking from the National Speakers Association.

Theodore Roosevelt was the twenty-sixth president of the United States. He changed the way Americans view the presidency, making character development as important as policy.

Babe Ruth is considered to be one of the best baseball players of all time. He established MLB records for career home runs, runs batted in, bases on balls, slugging percentage, and on-base plus slugging.

Carl Sagan was an American scientist and popular science author best known for his research on extraterrestrial life. He received a vast number of awards, including honors from NASA, the American Astronautical Society, the Soviet Cosmonauts Federation and the National Academy of Sciences.

Antoine de Saint-Exupéry was a French poet and aviator. He was best known for his novella, *Le Petit Prince* (*The Little Prince*). He won the US National Book Award and several of France's highest literary prizes.

Robert Schuller was a pastor, motivational speaker, and author who broadcasted a weekly television program *Hour of Power* from the Crystal Cathedral for 40 consecutive years (1970–2010).

Albert Schweitzer was a German/French theologian, medical missionary, and philosopher known for his historical work on Jesus. He received the Nobel Peace Prize in 1952.

William Shakespeare is widely considered as the greatest English writer in history. His use of words shaped modern English; he invented many words and expressions that are common today.

William Joseph Slim was a British military commander who published writing under the pen name Anthony Mills. A number of buildings and streets are named after him.

Socrates was a classical Greek philosopher credited as one of the founders of Western philosophy.

Roger Staubach was an American soldier and an extremely successful professional football player. He was the MVP of Super Bowl VI and was named to the Pro Bowl six times.

W. Clement Stone was a self-help author who rose from poverty to riches by focusing on maintaining a positive mental attitude.

Jonathan Swift was a British/Irish satirist and political writer. Many of his works are still read and taught today, notably *Gulliver's Travels* and *A Modest Proposal.*

Charles Swindoll is an evangelical Christian pastor and radio personality. He is the author of more than 70 books, and his radio program *Insight for Living* is broadcast on more than 2,000 stations in 15 languages.

Brian Tracy is a self-help expert in personal development. He has written more than 70 books, consulted for more than 1,000 companies, and addresses more than 250,000 people a year as a keynote speaker.

Ralph Waldo Trine was a philosopher and author who belonged to the New Thought movement of philosophy. He wrote over a dozen books.

Mark Twain, born Samuel Langhorne Clemens, was an American author and humorist. William Faulkner called him "the father of American literature." He is best known for his books *Adventures of Huckleberry Finn* and *The Adventures of Tom Sawyer.*

Leonardo da Vinci was an Italian artist and inventor who made great contributions to diverse fields including science, art, mathematics and architecture. He is best known as the artist behind the *Mona Lisa, The Last Supper* and the *Vitruvian Man.*

Voltaire, born François-Marie Arouet, was a French writer and satirist who advocated freedom of religion and expression, and the separation of church and state. He wrote in almost every form, including over 20,000 letters and over 2,000 books and pamphlets.

Booker T. Washington was a leader in the African-American community in the early 20th century. He was the first African-American to be pictured on a postal stamp, and schools, parks and a ship have been named after him.

George Washington was one of the Founding Fathers of the United States and unanimously elected its first president. Renowned for his leadership skills and military strategy, Washington is consistently ranked in the top three presidents in American history.

Oprah Winfrey is a talk show host, North America's only black billionaire, and according to several assessments, the most influential woman in the world.

Coach John Wooden was an American basketball player and extremely successful coach. He has the best winning record in NCAA history, leading his team at UCLA to 10 NCAA championships in 12 years.

William Butler Yeats was an Irish writer and senator. He helped advance the Irish Literary Revival and was awarded the Nobel Prize in Literature in 1923.

Zig Ziglar, born Hilary Hinton Ziglar, was an American motivational speaker and the author of a number of self-help books. He traveled the United States and the world giving speeches for more than 40 years. At his busiest, he was speaking 150 times a year.

ABOUT THE AUTHOR

Eamonn Percy has more than 25 years of business experience in helping companies transform and grow. He is a problem-solver, advisor, investor, board member, author and speaker on the topics of business growth and leadership. He is the Founder and President of The Percy Group Capital + Business Advisors, a leading business performance improvement firm that helps determined business leaders permanently solve problems, accelerate performance and get results.

Eamonn knows how to overcome obstacles, as he literally went from a stock room to the boardroom, from a midnight shift production supervisor to an executive with leading global companies, from being broke and sleeping in his car to owning a historic ranch, from being a C student in high school to completing an electrical engineering degree and an MBA. He understands the real-life struggles people face each day and knows how to help people overcome those struggles.

Eamonn has held a variety of technical, management and senior leadership roles with global companies in the technology, manufacturing, engineering, energy and professional services sectors, including Ford Electronics (now part of Visteon), Pirelli Cables, Ballard Power Systems and Powertech Labs. He has a B Eng (Electrical) from Lakehead University and an MBA (Finance) from the University of Toronto (Rotman School of Management). He has significant board experience in the commercial, academic and regulatory sectors, and is an award recipient for Professional Development and Career Achievement.

What makes Eamonn different is his pragmatic approach to business growth based on his unique combination of technical, business and leadership skills, plus his real-life experience in actually running companies.

He is passionate about performance improvement and encourages people to leave no stone unturned in their pursuit of big goals, great results and making a lasting impact.

Eamonn lives in Vancouver, BC, Canada.

DID YOU ENJOY
THE 1% SOLUTION?

Thank you for purchasing this book.

If you enjoyed reading it, please take a moment to leave a review online, so that you may inspire others to read this book and improve their lives as well.

Your feedback is much appreciated and will help me write better books, in order to fulfill my mission of helping people achieve their true potential.

CONTACT INFORMATION

EAMONN PERCY

#196 – 5525 West Boulevard

Vancouver, British Columbia,

Canada, V6M 3W6

604-261-6216

Email: epercy@percygroup.ca

LinkedIn: linkedin.com/in/eamonnpercy

Twitter: @EamonnPercy

Website: percygroup.ca

Contact The Percy Group Capital + Business Advisors

For more information on how to accelerate the growth of your business
visit us at percygroup.ca.

Subscribe to our free weekly newsletter and receive real-life business
resources, tactics and actions on how to accelerate the growth of your
business, by visiting percygroup.ca.

Made in the USA
Lexington, KY
21 June 2019